THE
FEARSOME
DILEMMA:
SIMULTANEOUS
INFLATION
AND
UNEMPLOYMENT

BY ALEX N. McLEOD

UNIVERSITY
PRESS OF
AMERICA

LANHAM • NEW YORK • LONDON

Copyright © 1984 by

University Press of America,™ Inc.

4720 Boston Way
Lanham, MD 20706

3 Henrietta Street
London WC2E 8LU England

Library of Congress Cataloging in Publication Data

McLeod, Alex N., 1911-
  The fearsome dilemma.

  Bibliography: p.
  Includes index.
  1. Unemployment—Effect of inflation on—History—20th
century. I. Title.
HD5710.M35 1985   331.13'72   84-26960
ISBN 0-8191-4519-X (alk. paper)
ISBN 0-8191-4520-3 (pbk. : alk. paper)

All University Press of America books are produced on acid-free
paper which exceeds the minimum standards set by the National
Historical Publications and Records Commission.

ACKNOWLEDGEMENTS

Surely the first debts an author must acknowledge are to his family, his teachers, and his colleagues and former colleagues. It may be invidious to single out individuals in these categories, but I must make special mention of my wife Rosalind for continuous aid and encouragement throughout my career. Among my teachers I am most conscious of my debts to Dean Matheson and to Professors F.A. Knox and W.A. Mackintosh at Queen's University in the 1930's and to Professors A.H. Hansen, J.A. Schumpeter, and J.H. Williams at Harvard from 1945 to 1947. Among my former colleagues at the International Monetary Fund I particularly value the example set by E.M. Bernstein as a conscientious and able international civil servant, the pleasure of working with the late George A. Blowers in Libya and Saudi Arabia, and later the sympathetic interest of Frank A. Southard Jr.

Some of the material in the pages that follow has already appeared elsewhere, sometimes in almost exactly the same form of words. Some of the comments made in a paper entitled "Reform of the International Monetary System and the Interests of the Developing Countries", presented in February 1970 to a colloquium organized by the Committee on Society, Development, and Peace (SODEPAX), anticipate certain passages in Chapter 1 and elsewhere; the paper was included in *Money in a Village World*, Geneva, SODEPAX, 1970. Some of the ideas in other passages appeared in "The Essential Conditions for International Economic Stability", *Banca Nazionale del Lavoro Quarterly Review*, No. 113, June 1975; in "The Fearsome Dilemma: Simultaneous Inflation and Unemployment", the same journal, No. 131, December 1979; in "Reforming the International Monetary System", first published in Spanish in the Centro de Estudios Monetarios Latinoamericanos's *Boletin* for January-February 1982, then in English in the *International Journal of Social Economics*, Vol. 10, no. 2, 1983; in "Wanted: A Better Anti-Inflation Strategy", *Queen's Quarterly* [Kingston, Canada], Spring 1983; in "Fairer Income Taxes", *Policy Options*, [Halifax, Canada,] Vol. 5, no. 1, January 1984; and in "Regressive Budgets Won't Cure Inflation", to be published in a forthcoming issue of the same journal.

The manuscript was conscientiously prepared for typesetting by James S. Hill of Richvale Telecommunications Ltd.

CONTENTS

PREFACE

First, a word to those whom I expect to be the principal readers of this book: members of the general public without much specialized knowledge of economics but who are comfortable with serious newspapers like the London *Times* or the New York *Times* or the Toronto *Globe and Mail;* and undergraduate students in economics and related disciplines, who may find it a useful supplement to standard economics textbooks.

I have tried to keep the presentation simple and readable, but I do not suppose I have completely succeeded. Nevertheless I do not apologize for including some passages that may be a little more abstruse or tightly-argued than you would like, for they may stimulate you to dig a little deeper. To aid in readability the footnotes have been divided into two classes. Those that expand on or illuminate the material in the main text are identified by asterisks or daggers or the like, and are placed at the foot of the page. Those that give the source of a citation or allusion are identified by numbers, and will be found under References at the end of the book. For the most part these references have been selected for clarity and simplicity rather than for comprehensive treatment or depth of analysis, though some are more difficult than others. I have also included a few that are really addressed to the professional economist, with a warning note that they are more technical.

* * *

Next, some comments addressed not only to those same readers but also to professional economists, or at least those of them who choose to thumb through the book in search of new ideas to explore or errors to correct or whatever. You should be warned that I approach my subject from the point of view of an unregenerate reformer. My interest in things economic began as an adolescent on the Canadian Prairies in the 1920's, puzzled by the apparent discrepancies between the fortunes of the primary producers who worked the Western grain fields and those of others in towns and cities farther East who seemed to reap most of the material rewards, though I was then entirely innocent of the science of economics. (I remember a perverse sense of pleasure when I first reached Kingston in the fall of 1930 to attend Queen's University; I saw the vast grain fleets tied up idle, and rejoiced that the downstream elements in the wheat economy were suffering too!) But my serious interest in economics began when The Great Depression prematurely terminated my intended career in mathematics and physics. My twin brother Gordon and I were fortunate enough to land jobs in the Canadian Civil Service in

Ottawa, saved money, and returned to Queen's to study economics. We wanted to know what had hit us, and what could be done about it.

From that time on my interest in economics has been in the contribution it can make to practical policymaking in Canada and in the world at large, for the benefit of the general citizenry. I heartily agree with the late Professor John Williams of Harvard that policymaking is the basic purpose of economic studies. I therefore have little patience with the direction in which many economists are now directing their efforts, especially but not solely in the academic sphere. Some are studiously ignoring the important policy problems that urgently need attention but are so difficult to deal with, and are vigorously pursuing unimportant problems they feel they **can** deal with. (If you think I am joking, just flip over the pages of any of the many journals that still claim to be addressed to economics: they are filled with brief articles more concerned with the application of mathematical and econometric techniques than with economics.) Others have cheerfully thrown over all we have painfully learned since the 1930's and are busy jumping off one bandwagon onto another in a vain effort to keep up with the crowd acclaiming the latest economic guru, instead of doing serious thinking of their own.

In the 1950's and 1960's the economics profession was taken seriously by politicians and by the public, for we graciously accepted the credit for solving the problems of deflation and unemployment, though the credit really belonged to only a few original thinkers among our numbers. The profession would dearly like to be taken seriously again, but it is only making an ass of itself instead. Few professional economists today are focusing clearly on the inflation-unemployment dilemma, though it is surely the most pressing policy issue of the day, whereas their predecessors of an earlier generation were deeply involved in seeking remedies for The Great Depression.

It is of course true that the remedies that seemed to be working in the 1950's and 1960's have faltered, and the high hopes of those years have been dashed; maintaining high levels of employment at stable prices has proven more difficult than we thought. However, that is reason to seek improvements in our techniques, not to throw out everything that we have learned in the last 50 years and go back to the techniques of the 1920's... or the 1870's... or even earlier. Suppose a group of engineers had designed a bridge and had started to build it, only to discover that the ground below a column supporting the ends of two spans had been inadequately explored and would not carry the weight intended. Would they give up on the project, throw the completed spans into the river, and advise the public to go back to using ferries and fords instead of bridges? Or would they seek alternative ways of completing the structure? Well, what should economists do in a similar situation, if they really want to be considered a profession?

* * *

My concern with inflation goes a long way back. In the 1945-1946 academic year I presented a paper to the Hansen-Williams fiscal policy seminar at Harvard University, arguing against the popular view that a mild inflation would stimulate investment and thus promote prosperity. I said this attempt to fool people for their own good would fail, because they would soon recognize what was going on and adjust their behavior accordingly. I advocated letting the expected annual increases in productivity bring a gradual reduction in prices, instead of providing increased wages and other factor returns; that would let everyone share the benefits, instead of only those working in the industries that were growing fastest. I think I was the only member of the seminar so persuaded.

When I came to Toronto in 1955 and found that my new colleagues around the luncheon table at The Toronto-Dominion Bank were cheerfully agreed that prices would continue to rise at 1 or 2 percent per annum indefinitely, my concern about creeping inflation rose sharply; I have ever since bent the ear of everyone who would listen (not many) in an effort to convert them. At that time prices in the U.S.A. and some other countries were being boosted by the Korean War. A little later unemployment breached the 3 percent level that was widely considered to be the boundary of full employment, so the problem of simultaneous inflation and unemployment had reared its head even then. One economist was prompted to call such a situation an economist's hell on earth. Well, what would he say now, after both rates have tested the double-digit range in many countries?

Toronto Canada   A.N.M.
July 1984

Part One ————————

DIAGNOSIS

Chapter 1
THE ATTRIBUTES OF INFLATION

The Meaning of Inflation

Most countries nowadays face an apparently-intractable policy dilemma in that they have higher levels of both inflation and unemployment than they are prepared to accept, but presently-employed techniques for reducing one make the other worse, so they are unable to achieve a satisfactory performance in either field, let alone both at once. This phenomenon may be called The Fearsome Dilemma, because it seems so widespread and so severe. It is the major theme of this book. The principle focus will be on inflation as an independent problem, however, for two reasons. First, it is presently the major object of attention by policymakers in most countries. Second, we will argue in due course that it can be successfully attacked by means that do not make unemployment worse. That will solve the present policy dilemma and permit demand-management techniques to be effectively used to support high levels of output and employment, as they were with a substantial degree of success for two decades or more after World War II.

Inflation has been defined in different ways at different times as economic fashions have changed, but no matter how it has been defined its essential feature has always been rising prices. Nowadays, therefore, most economists define inflation as a persistent rise in the general price level. That includes the prices of the things we buy and consume regularly, like food and clothing; the rental we pay for housing accommodation or the costs homeowners incur in keeping a roof over their heads; the costs of operating our automobiles, admissions to movies and plays and concerts, the services of doctors and dentists and other professionals; and so on. Indeed, the rate of inflation is commonly measured by the behavior of a consumer-price index addressed to just these costs, because it gives a reasonably fair indication of the impact of inflation on a typical individual.

However, all sorts of other prices are also included, at both the consumer and the producer level. For the consumer, the general price level also includes the initial cost of durable goods, automobiles, and houses. For the producer, it includes wages and salaries, materials and supplies, financial costs, and other charges. Interest rates are prices too, whether paid by the consumer or the producer; they are the rental paid for the use of someone else's money for an agreed period of time. All these prices sooner or later are reflected in the consumer price index, but at any given moment they may be behaving somewhat differently; for some purposes, therefore, it is better to gauge inflation by a broader measure, such as the implicit price index or "deflator" derived from the gross national product (i.e. the value of all goods and services produced in the economy). This index is obtained by dividing the total product valued at current prices by the total valued at the prices of some previous year.

At some risk of labouring the obvious, we must emphasize that it would be a mistake to blame every increase in every price on inflation. The price mechanism plays an important part in helping to regulate production, consumption, and the allocation of productive resources, through a complex system of interrelated markets: the prices at which we sell our labour (wages and salaries) or the prices we get for the use of our invested capital (interest and similar investment returns) largely determine our incomes; how we choose to spend those incomes is strongly influenced by the prices we have to pay for various goods and services; those prices in turn depend largely on the cost of production; and production costs can ultimately be resolved into the wages of labour and returns to invested capital. In order for the price mechanism to perform these functions properly, some prices may have to rise or fall relative to others as conditions change; such relative price movements are **functional**, and do not imply either inflation or deflation, because increases here should be offset by decreases there.

Indeed, you may argue that a rise in the **general** price-level of a small country, or a particular geographic region within a larger country, may sometimes be functional rather than truly inflationary. For example, the sharp increase in world oil prices that began in 1974 prompted a substantial increase in the demand for coal and other sources of energy. Even if national price-levels had remained stable, there would probably have been a functional increase in the price of coal; this in turn might well have led to a rise in miners' wages and in the returns to invested capital in the coal-producing areas, especially if it had been necessary to attract additional labour and capital. The resultant increase in regional prosperity might well have permitted or encouraged higher prices, wages, and returns to capital throughout the coal-mining region; the implication is simply that the good fortune of the region was being shared by all or most residents. The rise in regional prices would presumably have been offset by weaknesses in prices elsewhere in the national economy.

The opposite of inflation is deflation: a persistent fall in the general price level. Deflation is associated in the public's mind with massive unemployment and idle productive capacity, as in the 1930's, but the two phenomena are logically quite distinct. That distinction is, unfortunately, heavily underlined by the fact that for some years now most of the world has been suffering from severe unemployment and idle productive capacity along with inflation. Nor is the end yet in sight. That, as we will soon see, is what makes today's inflation so hard to combat.

Adverse Effects

It is often said that the main evil of inflation is the erosion of the real incomes of those on fixed incomes, such as pensioners and annuitants. These people may indeed suffer seriously, but if that were the only problem it could be solved quite easily by tax-supported subsidies that would not impose any serious drain on the real income of the economy as a whole. In practice this is already done for many low-income groups, though with some lag and in a somewhat hit-or-miss fashion; the initial impact of inflation is probably regressive, but social-service payments tend to be periodically increased in response.

The most serious effects of inflation are the resulting distortions of the price mechanism, which as already noted is a major instrument of decisionmaking in a money-and-market economy. These distortions are systematic rather than random, so their effects tend to be cumulative. The distribution of real incomes is altered throughout the economy, not just for pensioners and annuitants, and altered in rather unpredictable and not necessarily functional ways. Most other aspects of decision-making are also distorted.

Persistent price rises increase the probability of labour strife, resulting in greater losses due to strikes and lockouts. The familiar vicious circle of prices and wages means that labour foresees the erosion of its real wages over the life of any wage contract and attempts to protect itself by demanding correspondingly larger annual increments in money wages, thereby helping to maintain the upward pressures on prices. These demands tend to escalate as it becomes clear that "nice guys finish last"— groups that accept relatively moderate settlements do not see any benefit in the prices they must pay for what they buy, and they see more ruthless groups faring better.

Many of the worst distortions resulting from inflation show themselves in the money and capital markets. It becomes obvious to both borrowers and lenders that a contract for the return of a fixed sum at the end of any but a quite short period of time will be paid off in money of less purchasing power than that lent, so lenders tend to ask (and borrowers have little grounds for refusing) a more-or-less offsetting increase in the rate of interest, i.e. an inflation premium, which we may suppose will approximate the rate at which prices are expected to rise over the term of the contract. Despite the inflation of nominal interest rates, however, it may become almost impossible to borrow beyond the short-term range except by the addition of "sweeteners" of some kind or other, such as rights to convert into equities. Also, different members of society are affected differently, especially if, as is usually the case, the typical lender must pay tax on the nominal rather than the real value of his interest earnings, and the typical borrower (or at least the typical business borrower) can deduct his interest payments from his income as a business expense. This combination of distortions means that the net real rate of interest after tax may well be negative for some borrowers or some lenders or both.

Inflation subsidizes the anticipation of needs for physical plant and equipment. This further intensifies current inflationary pressures, and may get capital "frozen in" to equipment that may become obsolescent before it begins to be effectively used. Once begun, capital projects are relatively insensitive to cost increases because the recovery of these costs will be spread over several years' operations. If a boom develops, capital costs may increase further as contractors become fully booked and can only be induced to take on more work if the terms are suitably generous. Oddly enough, the construction industry is in danger of being the chief victim instead of the chief beneficiary in such instances: most projects take at least several months to complete, some take several years, and rising costs can bankrupt a contractor unless he takes care to protect himself through escalation clauses and the like. However, despite the hidden subsidy to the cost of borrowing, it does not appear in practice that inflation ensures a vigourous volume of capital formation: doubts, uncertainties, industrial disputes, bottlenecks, and physical shortages seem to conspire against such an outcome.

Even though nominal interest rates may rise sharply, real interest rates (i.e. after adjusting for inflation) may remain low for a considerable time. The inflation premium in nominal rates may be materially less than the rate of inflation, for a variety of reasons. From the 1950's to the 1970's the officials responsible for fiscal and monetary policies in most countries actively pursued inappropriately-low interest rates in an effort to stimulate employment,* either because they did not fully appreciate the distortions thus introduced into the economy or because they consid-

---

* At least one Canadian economist was advocating more realistic interest rates in the middle 1950's, by which time it was pretty clear that the risk of relapse into depression was remote and the reality of creeping inflation was obvious. His was a voice crying in the wilderness. Name on request.

ered them less damaging than the effects of the alternative policies available to them. The public took a long time to shed "the money illusion", i.e. the illusion that money income and real income are the same. Even when this illusion fades, as it has pretty well done by now, nominal interest rates may not fully reflect the rate of inflation because it will be difficult to forecast future price trends accurately and because there will be serious constraints on the freedom of action of some borrowers (and to some extent on some lenders as well).

Take the case of a young couple with limited capital resources who wish to buy a home in which to raise their family. For starters, both they and the people they hope to buy a house from will realize that its value is likely to appreciate over time if inflation continues; however, the seller will not be able to capitalize this expectation in full, for the very practical reason that the buyer will be unlikely to be able to get a mortgage loan big enough to cover the expected value of the house ten or twenty or thirty years later.* Next, it is true that the couple's money income, and therefore their ability to meet the mortgage payments, will **probably** rise more or less in step with inflation as the years go by, and that the value of the house will **probably** rise correspondingly (unless the rate of inflation has been overestimated) and thereby give them a capital profit when they eventually come to sell the house that will **probably** offset a significant portion of the high interest rates they will be paying in the meantime. But all that is of no help to them at the time of purchase: they must pay the interest and amortization of the loan out of their current income, not the income they hope to have some day. This puts a serious constraint on the size of the mortgage loan they can afford, and therefore on the price they can afford to pay for a house. Nor can they escape these costs by renting instead of buying, because their rental payments must cover the same costs for their landlord with not even a hope of eventually recouping some portion of it through a capital gain. Indeed, the prospects of continuing inflation may lead them to buy even when they would be better off renting, thereby reducing their mobility if an attractive employment opportunity were to occur in another part of the country.

Farmers, fishermen, and the owners of small businesses face essentially similar problems in finding the necessary capital to start a new venture or to expand an existing one.

An established business with a good record of profitability has important advantages in raising capital in any circumstances, especially if it is large enough and well-enough known to win acceptance for its issues in

---

* It follows that any attempt to help buyers meet the cost of a new home will probably be passed on to the sellers in the form of higher prices.

the capital market. Under inflationary conditions such enterprises, too, will face having to replace their existing capital facilities at higher costs in due course, but in the meantime their cash flows will rise and the interest costs of adding to their plant and equipment are deductible as a business expense from current taxable income; for the time being at least, the tax collector subsidizes their expansion plans, whether in the form of new capital outlays or in the form of buying out other going concerns. In principle they must eventually pay additional taxes on the income generated by their new productive facilities thus financed, but there is an old adage that "tax postponed is tax forgone": at the very least, they will have had the interest-free use of funds equal to the taxes thus deferred. Hence inflation tends to accentuate the advantages of large established firms over new ventures.

More generally, inflation interferes with the efficient allocation of economic resources, which is a major function of the pricing system. Even a relatively mild creeping inflation makes virtually all business activity look more profitable than it really is, thereby weakening the necessary and normal pressure towards improved efficiency and the weeding out of the incompetent. The accounting profession has been struggling for years to devise techniques and procedures that would eliminate inflationary biases from operating statements and balance sheets, with only limited success.

All these distortions have become more and more painfully evident as the decade of the 1970's has given way to that of the 1980's. The prime lending rate of commercial banks in many countries has risen above 20 percent at times, with mortgage and other long-term rates not far behind. The results have been particularly painful to homeowners, who had been encouraged by the unrealistically-low nominal interest rates of the previous 30 years or so into bidding house prices up to inflated levels and taking on purchase commitments that have suddenly become unexpectedly burdensome when mortgage loans come up for renegotiation. They have also been encouraged to buy more commodious and sumptuous quarters than they might have done if they had realized the real rate of interest they would eventually have to pay, not only on their mortgages but also on the capital expenditures on roads, water and sewer facilities, and other services financed out of real-estate taxes. Farmers and other small businesses, too, were misled into similarly-heavy capital commitments by the lure of apparently-cheap borrowed capital.

Perhaps the most serious distortion of all, however, is the threat that inflation poses for the monetary-and-fiscal-policy mechanism that gave us 20 or 30 years of prosperity after World War II and is still our best hope for sustained progress. Expansive policies require the placement of interest-bearing instruments in willing hands, including the hands of banks and other financial intermediaries, in the form of **either** private borrowings induced by easy-money policies **or** public issues to support fiscal measures. Contractive policies involve the absolute or relative shrinkage of the public's holdings of money-proper and other very liquid assets, and can be more delicately adjusted if the public can be induced to take up less-liquid longer-term securities in exchange for monetary assets or shorter-term securities without demanding too large an increase in yields. Of course contraction can also be effected by a sufficiently-large government surplus and the net reduction of government issues outstanding, but even this will not save the government from the need to meet the redemption schedules of its maturing debt: so much of it is at short term nowadays that not even savagely-repressive surpluses could avoid the need to roll over a substantial portion of most maturities. A successful policy of restraint must therefore depend on the willingness of the public to buy bonds; and serious difficulty in effecting a necessary contraction smoothly may make the financial intermediaries and the general public less ready to participate in the next expansion.

Evidently we must have **both** price stability **and** full employment, or we may end up with neither.

What Rate of Inflation Can Be Tolerated?

While they lasted, most of the inflations that occurred before World War II seemed to be associated with prosperity, full employment, and boom times—especially the more moderate inflations. Not surprisingly, many people were thereby led to advocate either deliberate inflations of moderate proportions or financial policies that would have had inflationary effects; the advocates of the free coinage of silver in the U.S.A. during the closing years of the 19th century are a conspicuous example. In some cases the supporters of such policies were businessmen and other debtors who would have benefitted directly (businessmen are typically net borrowers, and borrowers tend to benefit at the expense of lenders in times of inflation), but others were motivated by considerations of the general welfare of the economy. However, most of the advantages are illusory. The benefits from an inflation-fed boom are likely to be frustrated by bottlenecks, material shortages, high interest rates, and other adverse side effects. And of course the clinching argument is the almost-world-wide experience since the 1960's: inflation has not brought prosperity.

During The Great Depression of the 1930's a few bold souls advocated combatting deflation with moderate doses of inflation, which they named "reflation" in order to make it sound more respectable. Nowadays few economists would dispute the basic validity of that prescription, though they would probably translate it into the terminology of demand management (then unknown) and would want to offer fairly specific prescriptions for how it should be done most efficiently and with least risk of overkill. These proposals were summarily rejected by the authorities in most countries on the grounds that they might lead to uncontrollable inflation—despite the fact that the problem of the time was clearly a serious and apparently uncontrollable deflation! We must remind ourselves, however, that "reflation" was then seen, not in the light of today's demand-management theories, but as the weakening if not the actual rejection of the then-standard precepts of monetary orthodoxy, i.e. the convertibility of all credit-based (or paper) money into gold or its equivalent. Virtually every previously-known attempt of this kind had ended in disaster. Furthermore, considering that the creeping inflation that worried us in the 1950's became a cantering inflation in the 1970's and is stoutly resisting severe countermeasures in the 1980's, can we really say that the authorities' fears of reflation in the 1930's were entirely unjustified?

A more dubious argument for "moderate" inflation was popular as World War II came to an end, and helped to entrench the price trends that now bedevil us. Looking back at the 1930's, and fearing that deflation would again become chronic before long, some economists advocated a deliberate gentle inflation as a device for stimulating the economy. A few voices objected that the rate of inflation would tend to accelerate (they said, "A little inflation is like a little pregnancy, it tends to grow!"), or that the public would soon come to recognize the pattern and therefore its stimulating effect would be discounted, but the idea that inflation of "only" one or two percent a year would be beneficial or at least harmless gained wide acceptance. History seems to have vindicated the critics.

As a **policy goal**, then, it is hard to see much merit in any rate of inflation above zero—perhaps as an average over a number of years, not necessarily an absolute figure for every year individually. Indeed, purists may argue that the ideal should be a steady **decline** in prices to reflect the (presumably continuing) benefits of new technology and other factors in improving the productivity of the economy, and to ensure that all members of society share equitably in those benefits. Perfection is not of this world, however, so as a practical matter we may have to accept a **standard of actual performance** that falls short of that goal. If we are prepared to do so, what would be the upper limit to the rate of inflation we should be prepared to tolerate?

If economic policymakers could focus exclusively on the general price level, inflation would be no problem: the tolerable upper level might be zero. The authorities could not prevent temporary fluctuations, of course, but on the average over quite short periods of time they could enforce whatever general trend they chose; by a judicious combination of tight money and high taxes they could put a ceiling on the rate of increase or even impose a decrease, and by an easier monetary policy and fiscal intervention they could prevent or limit any decline. In practice, however, policymakers must simultaneously pursue at least two other major economic goals besides price stability: a high level of employment and output, and a viable balance of payments. (A viable balance of payments may be defined as a combination of the ability of the economy to earn its way in world trade in the medium and long term with the ability to contain short-term fluctuations in its external reserves and in the exchange rate of its currency within internationally-acceptable limits.) The issues thus raised will be pursued later at some length, especially in the second section of Chapter 7, where it will be argued that the proper focus is on the two domestic goals. We are thus led back to the policy dilemma with which we introduced this chapter.

In recent years the popular approach has been to see the problem in terms of a relatively simple trade-off between the two horns of The Fearsome Dilemma: at what point do the evils of a little more inflation just balance the evils of a little less unemployment? Unfortunately there are at least three serious faults with this approach. First, economists have been squabbling for years (with no signs of reaching agreement) over whether there really is such a trade-off at all, and if so whether it is a short-run thing, a long-run thing, or neither, and whether it is a stable or an unstable relationship. Second, while economists squabbled the trade-off (if that is what it is) got decidedly worse: 3 or 4 percent unemployment and 1 or 2 percent inflation in the 1950's moved into the double-digit range for both horns of the dilemma in the 1980's, with disappointing improvement by mid-decade. Third, even if a trade-off could be found that was relatively stable and reasonably acceptable to the general public at some given time, it would surely not remain permanently acceptable as a long-term goal. The public, quite properly, may be expected to demand progressively greater success in respect of both goals.

Thus the trade-off approach offers no real answer to what is a tolerable rate of inflation. To face the question squarely, I do not see any clear basis for that decision. Any inflation is bad, and more is worse than less, but I am unable to identify any critical rate above which the harmful effects become categorically worse than at a somewhat lower rate. It is conceivable that empirical studies could identify a critical rate in this sense, below which economic decisionmakers do not take account of inflation in an appreciable way but above which they do; however, if there is such a rate then I would guess it would be so far below the rates that obtain today among the principal trading nations of the world as to be indistinguishable from zero for all practical purposes.

It is still true, as some critics of the then-orthodox economic policies of the 1930's used to say, that "What is physically possible ought to be financially possible": there is no obvious logical contradiction between the goals of price stability and high levels of employment, though there are certainly practical difficulties in attaining them simultaneously. There are clear if imprecise limits to the level to which unemployment can be reduced—frictional problems, seasonal problems, structural problems, and so on—but there are no obviously-insurmountable obstacles to achieving approximate price stability.

Chapter 2
LESSONS FROM THE PAST

Convertibility

Prior to World War II (1939-1945) **recognized** inflations were relatively rare, and for the most part were independent local phenomena peculiar to a particular country, though of course wide-ranging disturbances such as a major war might lead to more-or-less-simultaneous inflations in several countries. However, there were many **unrecognized** inflations—unrecognized at the time, at least, though modern economists certainly recognize them for what they were. In part this is because until compara-tively recent times the available statistical techniques and factual data were not adequate to identify moderate movements in the general price level with any accuracy. But a more important part of the explanation lies in the limitations of older theories of money and what gives money value, which you should be warned about in case you decide to read up on what economists of an earlier day had to say about inflation in general or about particular instances.

Nowadays most monetary economists recognize that the readiness of a seller to accept whatever passes for "money" where he lives is largely dependent on his confidence that it will be readily accepted by other sellers in their turn when he wishes to use it to buy their wares: as we will soon see, people will continue for a long time to accept even a money whose purchasing power is clearly declining, and only try to reject it when the rate of decline becomes very rapid indeed. Before the collapse of the gold standard in the 1930's, however, most economists firmly believed that what gave money its value was its bullion content (as in full-weight gold or silver coins) or its ready convertibility either directly or indirectly into bullion. They clung to that view despite considerable evidence to the contrary, and indeed vestiges of their quaint belief can still be found today. Even in the days before paper money, most trade was quite satisfactorily conducted by the use of monetary counters that did not contain the amount of bullion they were supposed to, but were clipped, hollowed, "sweated", or otherwise lightened. The acceptance of paper money was "explained" by its technical convertibility into gold, though the fallacy of that notion was amply demonstrated every time the public tried to convert any substantial portion: convertibility was promptly suspended, whereupon business continued to be conducted as usual with the now-inconvertible paper money. The experts loftily explained that in such circumstances the paper money retained its value because of the **expectation** that convertibility would be restored in due course.

It is certainly true that many inconvertible paper currencies were sooner or later discredited by inflationary excesses. The point is that convertibility was a reasonably-effective **control mechanism** for the volume of money in circulation, not that it "gave value" to it in some mysterious way. It proved to be by no means a perfect control mechanism, which is why the switch to "managed money" was made in the 1920's (an attempt to manage the price level, and thereby the business cycle, by regulating the money supply) and the further switch to "demand management" after World War II. And it is certainly clear that these management techniques are still far from perfect; in fact they have been pretty well discredited in the public's mind, though quite improperly so, as this book will strongly argue.

Given the plentiful examples of inflations linked to inadequately-controlled issues of inconvertible paper money, it is not surprising that economists of an earlier day often **defined** the phenomenon either as a disproportionate increase in the money supply or as recourse to an inconvertible fiat money. They saw sharply-rising prices as the **result** of inflation so defined, and they often measured the inflation by the depreciation of the currency in terms of gold or in terms of currencies that continued to be convertible into gold. (Exchange-rate statistics were more easily available than price statistics, and more up-to-date; in principle a currency "ought" to depreciate about in step with inflation, but in practice the depreciation usually goes faster because inflation generates a flight of capital that depresses the exchange value of the currency more rapidly than domestic prices are rising.) They certainly noticed that prices rose and fell for other reasons as well, but usually much more moderately; they saw these movements as part of the business cycle, and did not consider price rises inflationary unless the canons of monetary orthodoxy had been breached.

Sixteenth-Century Europe

Let's look at a few examples of past inflations—especially the more spectacular ones, for they bring out some important points. Commonly the instrument of inflation was a paper currency-note or a banknote issued in disregard for the principles of convertibility. However, the first major inflation of modern times in the North Atlantic basin involved full-bodied gold and silver coins with no credit-money component at all:

it arose from the inflow of treasure into Europe soon after the discovery of the New World by Europeans. It was atypical in another respect as well, namely that it affected pretty much the whole of Europe simultaneously. Most of the treasure came to Spain initially, but it was rapidly redistributed by the normal processes of trade. Western Hemisphere gold was reaching the mints in Britain and other countries in some quantity by 1515, but silver soon became more important, especially after the opening of rich Bolivian mines in 1545 and Mexican mines soon after. Much of the bullion was promptly minted into coin and put into circulation. Silver coins were the money of the people, along with subsidiary copper coins, for gold coins were too valuable to be useful except for relatively large transactions, so the greater inflow of silver was doubly significant.

This experience is generally credited with giving rise to the first clear expression of what has come to be known as the quantity theory of money, in its crudest form: the price level varies with the quantity of money available for effecting a given volume of transactions. The addition of the concept of the velocity of circulation of money (i.e. how rapidly each unit of money is spent on the average) about a hundred years later greatly improved the theory, and gave it a place in the structure of theoretical economics which it retained until the 1930's. (For a brief explanation of the theory see section 4 of the Appendix). To this day it is still the best available framework for analyzing the effects of the more-or-less-mechanical injection of new money in an otherwise-stable situation (or at a faster rate than real output can grow). Indeed it is still commonly used to explain the broad sweep of any inflation, even those in which more complex lines of causation can be seen, though it has long been discredited as an explanation of deflations (since output and employment are more likely to decline than prices). Furthermore a somewhat modified version has evolved into the theoretical framework propounded by modern "monetarists" like Milton Friedman, who have made important contributions to our understanding of monetary phenomena. We will discuss some of their views later.

A number of similar though much milder and briefer episodes can be identified in the 19th century, due to the discovery of new gold fields in California (1848), Australia (1851), and the Klondike (1898), and the introduction of the cyanide process for extracting gold (1887). The increase in monetary gold in these cases was much smaller in relative terms than in the 16th century, but the multiple expansion of credit-money on a given gold base magnified the effects on the world money supply.

Moderate Inflations

Most major inflations have involved paper currencies or credit-based monies that either ceased to be convertible into gold (or silver or the like) at fixed rates or were issued from the first as fiat monies with no promise of redemption in any other form. The popular stereotype of such inflations is a flood of printing-press money, but of course a substantial portion of the money supply may take the form of deposit-money or cheque-book money. During the German inflation of the early 1920's, for example, commercial deposits at banks ranged from about 100 to about 130 percent of the note circulation, not much below the 1913 ratio of 159 percent,[1] though it is the expansion of the note issue that has got most of the attention. Paper monies of all kinds are so easily and cheaply expanded—their supply is so elastic—that a virtually-unlimited expansion is possible once the situation gets out of hand. However, an inconvertible paper currency does not necessarily lead to inflation, and when it does the inflation does not inevitably accelerate. There are examples of relative price stability for long periods under inconvertible monies, and some South American countries have had more-or-less continuous inflation for 100 years or more without lapsing into hyperinflation.

Inflations have commonly been linked to times of war or revolution, and to the financing of government deficits, but that is not true of them all. There are many examples of peacetime inflations associated with the growth of banking and the expansion of bank loans to businesses, but one will suffice. For reasons that need not detain us here, the public in Britain became more willing to accept and use paper money by the early years of the 18th century than in most other countries, and a great expansion of bank credit began. The Bank of England had been established a few years earlier and had been given a monopoly of the note issue in and around London, but the bulk of the banking business came to be performed by smaller deposit-taking banks in London and by private note-issuing banks in the rest of the country. Until mid-century the resulting monetary expansion seems to have served to finance a substantial expansion of trade without serious inflationary effects, as Britain was rapidly industrializing. In the second half of the century, however, a price rise began that eventually led into and merged with that associated with the Napoleonic Wars. The government was an important borrower, thanks to a series of wars in Europe and North America, but followed reasonably sound financial practices; most of the inflation may be ascribed to business borrowing to finance investment in industry and transportation.

Nevertheless it is clear that a major factor in many of the more spectacular inflations has been the use of monetary expansion to finance government deficits. In a few cases inflation has been a deliberate policy choice, as when a revolutionary government has used this technique to despoil a former *rentier* class, or when an invading army has used an issue of inconvertible currency to finance its activities at the expense of the vanquished population. In other cases a weak or inept or irresponsible government has been at fault. More typically, however, it has been some major disturbance or calamity that has led the government to resort to financial practices it would normally eschew, as being the lesser of two evils. Major wars provide the prime examples here: even in World War II, despite the fact that far more sophisticated fiscal techniques were available than in previous wars, inflations were general not only in belligerant nations but also in neutrals.

In principle it ought to be possible to finance all government expenditures either by taxes or by borrowing part of the public's voluntary savings out of current income, but at times that may be a counsel of perfection. In a typical modern state the governmental sector may absorb 20 or 25 percent of total real income (or total output) even in peacetime, not counting transfer payments made to some individuals out of taxes levied on others; mobilizing for a major war may easily double or triple that percentage, which means that personal consumption and business expenditures must be reduced correspondingly. This is not the place for a dissertation on war finance, but it is simply not feasible to quickly reduce the typical citizen's consumption of real goods and services that severely through increased taxation, which must of necessity be rather clumsy and can not take much account of every individual's circumstances. Housing accommodations offer a concrete example: any one family may materially reduce its expenditures by moving to smaller quarters, but there is no way that the size of all houses in the country (and the real costs of maintaining them) can be instantly reduced by say 25 percent and the difference channelled into financing the war effort.

Other misfortunes may bring problems that differ only in degree from those of war finance. Given sufficient time, pre-existing commitments and other inflexible claims on one's real income can indeed be sharply reduced, but wars and other major disturbances are usually not that accommodating. Monetary expansion to cover a deficit crowds the public out of the marketplace through what is in effect a flexible mixture of forced loans and taxation: the increase in money in circulation gives the government immediate command over additional goods and services in the same way that a voluntary loan would do, and any resulting increase in prices operates like a sales-tax on all purchases. Normal market forces then spread the effects gradually, though not necessarily fairly, among the members of the general public.

At first blush you might think that the end of hostilities would mean the end of wartime inflationary pressures, but that is not necessarily the case. The demobilization of the armed forces and the conversion of industrial production back to peacetime purposes may be a long and costly process. Countries that have been theatres of hostilities must undertake reconstruction that may assume daunting proportions. Defeated countries may be called on to make heavy reparations payments. Rationing, supply allocations, and other direct controls that have partly supplanted the price mechanism will be phased out, and the inflationary forces that have been partly suppressed thereby will be released. The patriotic pressure to reduce consumption and subscribe to war loans will abate, so people with money in their pockets and accumulated savings of various kinds will try to make up for long-unsatisfied demands for physical goods that may still be in short supply. Thus private demand will burgeon while government needs remain high. After World War I (1914-1918), for example, the peak of the inflation in Britain and the U.S.A. did not occur until 1920; in France and Italy, 1926; in most of Central Europe, somewhere in between those dates. After World War II much the same thing occurred, except that the period of rising prices never did come to a clear end, for reasons that are the subject matter of this book; at best they slowed to a creep for a while, then began to accelerate.

Continentals and *Assignats*

Two inflations in the late 18th century will start us on the history of the more spectacular instances. When thirteen of Britain's North American colonies rebelled in 1775 their revenue systems could not respond quickly to the increased expenditures necessitated by the War of Independence. They were already familiar with issues of paper money, and the individual colonies (or States) financed most of their additional activities by new issues. There was of course no true central government at first, only an assembly of State delegates called the Continental Congress, which had no proper taxing power and no real authority of its own. Neither domestic nor foreign loans were feasible initially; the Congress financed its activities by the issue of a paper money known as the Continental Currency from 1775 to 1779, though gold and silver coins remained in circulation, but by 1780 the new republic's finances were stabilized. The paper money depreciated little until the end of 1776, but rapidly thereafter; by mid-1781 it had ceased to pass and was traded by speculators at 1/500th to 1/1000th of its nominal value in silver—hence the phrase "not worth a Continental". The total issue was $242-million, some of which was accepted at a discount for a security issue in 1780 or otherwise redeemed. In 1790 an offer was made to redeem the remainder at 1/100th of its nominal value, but only about 70 percent of the amount believed outstanding was tendered; evidently the rest had been lost, or destroyed as worthless. The various State issues totalled $210-million, and most of these became virtually worthless as well.

The depreciation of the Continentals in the American Revolution was soon overshadowed by that of the *assignats* in the French Revolution. However, the problems that faced the *États Généraux* in 1789 were not those of war finance (though they were added later) but those of drastically revising the manifestly-unfair, inefficient, and deficit-ridden fiscal system it had inherited, compounded by an honourable but burdensome commitment to pay compensation for the feudal dues and certain other privileges it had abolished. Unjust taxes were repealed, but the disturbances of the times hampered the imposition and collection of new taxes. Lands confiscated from the king and the clergy were worth far more than the deficits envisaged before fiscal reforms could be completed, but any attempt to realize on them quickly by forced sales would have sacrificed much of their value.

The solution found was to sell *assignats* (literally, "writs of assignment"; in effect, a form of mortgage claim) which could be used in due course for the purchase of state lands. Soon the *assignats* were made legal tender. Those received in payment for land were duly destroyed, but land sales were effectively limited to some portion of the public's net savings out of current income, which was insufficient to cover the government's deficit, so new issues continued. War and civil disturbances in 1793 exacerbated the government's financial difficulties, prices (measured in *assignats*) rose, and the price-rise added to the financial problems: by the time tax payments fell due their real value had depreciated further, so the deficit worsened. Tax arrears were heavy, but hardly worth collecting in depreciated currency. Fiscal reforms were attempted from time to time, but proved ineffective. Eventually the government was able to regularize its receipts and payments in terms of coin (some coin remained in circulation most of the time, or was hoarded despite severe penalties) and the *assignats* were redeemed at about 1/3000th of their nominal value.

Continental Europe 1918-1924

The defeated Central Powers ended World War I with inflations of about the same order of magnitude as the victorious Allies and the neutrals. The various successor states suffered rather more inflation than Western Europe in the next few years, as might be expected, since they faced additional burdens: loss of territory, political reorganizations, looming reparations obligations, and so on. Even so, their inflations were relatively moderate until the middle of 1921. Leaving the case of Germany aside for the moment, the problem was particularly severe in Austria, Hungary, and Poland. Czechoslovakia did rather better, partly thanks to wise and vigourous policies but partly due to especially favourable circumstances: no devastated area, no war debts, no reparations obligations, and a strong industrial base. Finland and Latvia also got off lightly, having no war debts or reparations obligations. The experiences of the remainder were in between these extremes. The exchange values of all their currencies fell in sympathy with the mark in 1921, but some (including Austria) were stabilized as early as 1922, others (including Hungary and Poland) not till 1924. Most of these inflations were severe enough in their own right, though overshadowed by the German case. Writing in 1927, R.G. Hawtrey observed that the Austrian currency was stabilized at 1/14,400th of its former gold value.[2] He added tartly, "The figure looks respectable alongside the German or Russian ratio of depreciation. But in reality the advantage to a *rentier*, who formerly had £10,000 a year, of finding himself with 14s. a year rather than nothing is not very substantial."

The Russian rouble deserves a separate note, not so much because of the extent to which it lost purchasing power as because of an ideological element. Government revenues were disorganized after the revolution of November 1917, as one may well imagine, but spending requirements had to be met somehow. Even the most economically-orthodox of governments would probably have resorted to inflationary finance to some extent, but the new leaders anticipated the evolution of an economic system without money and therefore saw no reason to defend the purchasing power of the rouble they had inherited. Unrestricted monetary expansion generated an inflation that far exceeded those brought on by the Continentals and the *assignats*, bankrupted the *rentier* class, and destroyed the credit system. In 1921, however, the New Economic Policy abandoned the idea of a moneyless economic system and reintroduced certain forms of private enterprise and profits. A new rouble was eventually introduced in 1924, after several interim currency reforms, equal to 50-million old roubles.

The German Mark 1921-1923

As already noted, the inflation in Germany was of about the same order of magnitude as those of the other belligerents at the end of World War I; up till 1921 it was not particularly worse than elsewhere in Central Europe. The taxing powers of the new government were inadequate until December 1919, after which revenues were vigourously increased; the ordinary budget was in balance by 1921. Business borrowing from the banking system resumed, and became a material factor in monetary expansion. A socialist government had taken power two days before the armistice, and a number of reforms were introduced: the eight-hour day, recognition of labour unions, and an expanded social-insurance program. Employer and employee representatives worked out acceptable standards of fair wages that later played an important part in the course of the inflation: wage increases were linked to increases in the cost of living. Later, as inflation gathered momentum, wage adjustments were linked to the depreciation of the mark on foreign-exchange markets, so the depreciation of the mark was quickly reflected in wages and thus put immediate upward pressure on domestic prices. This was a common way of adjusting for inflation at the time, but it is likely to overcompensate, as noted in the first section of this chapter.

From the first there was no doubt that Germany would have to pay reparations, as France had been compelled to do at the end of the Franco-Prussian War. The terms of the Treaty of Versailles, signed in 1919, made it clear that the reparations would indeed be onerous, though it left the amount uncertain; obviously there would have to be a reduction in Germany's real income, including real wages, but the reformist (perhaps even revolutionary) spirit of the times and the "fair wage" compact with employers would make that difficult to achieve. By this time the government's ordinary budget was in or near balance, but no start had been made at generating a surplus out of which reparations could be paid. On 1st May 1921 the Reparations Commission reported; the amounts assessed were very large, they were expressed in terms of prewar gold marks, and substantial payments were to start at once. Whether or not it might eventually have been possible to raise taxes enough to cover the payments, it was clearly impossible to do so at once; domestic savings were insufficient to finance them by internal borrowing; external borrowing was not feasible in the international temper of the times; borrowing from the banking system (i.e. monetary expansion) was the only possibility for the time being at least. Inflation accelerated, and part way through 1922 wage settlements were linked to the depreciation of the mark. By this time prices were rising so fast that the real value of direct taxes fell appreciably between the time they were levied and the time they became payable.

In January 1923 France and Belgium occupied the Ruhr industrial area, on the grounds that promised coal deliveries (part of the reparations package) were not being made as agreed; the populace began a campaign of passive resistance; production and employment fell. The government assumed heavy new financial liabilities in support of the resistance, thus putting its budget clearly out of control. The public at last lost all semblance of confidence in the currency, hastened to spend it as soon as possible before its purchasing power declined even more, and eagerly bought any useful or useless physical object that might have some lasting value. In technical terms, hyperinflation or runaway inflation took over; the rapidly rising velocity of circulation vied with the rapidly rising volume of money to cover the skyrocketing nominal value of transactions. Pay periods were progressively shortened, till in the end wages were being paid twice a day.[3]

The end came came in the autumn. Reparations payments had been temporarily suspended. The government issued a new interim currency, the rentenmark, secured by a forced loan from industry and agriculture and linked to gold values more by promise than by actuality. The new issue worked because it gained public confidence and because government revenues and expenditures were stabilized in terms of it. In 1924 reparations payments were rescheduled under the Dawes Plan, and the rentenmark was replaced by a new permanent currency, the reichsmark.

The mechanics of the financial flows that generated the German inflation after 1921 are instructive. By that time the ordinary budget was more or less in balance, as already noted, but there was no surplus to apply to reparations. Once reparations payments were begun—and an ultimatum in May 1921 (the London Ultimatum) threatened severe penalties if they were not made—the German government had to enter the foreign-exchange market with marks to buy the foreign currencies that were required. Regardless of how it got the marks to do so, the result was to bid up the price of those currencies (i.e. to depreciate the mark); that raised the prices of exports and imports in terms of marks, and stimulated a parallel increase in domestic prices. The cost-of-living provisions of wage contracts meant that wages also rose promptly, including wages and salaries in the government sector; when wage adjustments were linked to the depreciation of the mark, this process accelerated. Rising domestic prices and wages added further to the government's deficit, and to the monetary expansion. Given the magnitude of the reparations payments, only very draconian fiscal measures could have broken this vicious circle; meantime, the inflation could only get worse. The flight of capital had already reached significant proportions, and accelerated sharply after the occupation of the Ruhr, offset to only a minor extent by speculators in other countries who bought marks in hopes they would eventually recover.

Lessons from the Past

It seems fair to summarize the lessons taught by past inflations in the following six points:

1. Inflation can arise even with a full-bodied commodity money or a money that remains fully convertible into a monetary commodity such as gold, but the potential for inflation is much greater with a paper or credit-based money.

2. Inflations, including major inflations, are likely to involve the expansion of deposit-money as well as currency-notes or banknotes, and may be generated by inadequately-controlled private borrowing just as readily as by inadequately-controlled government borrowing.

3. Inflation may be deliberately imposed by the authorities in pursuit of policy goals that may be social rather than economic, or may result from unwise policies, but most serious inflations have arisen because governments were faced with the urgent need to make expenditures that could not be financed by taxes or by voluntarily-raised loans. In such cases the recourse to inflationary financing may well be deemed a lesser evil than any feasible alternative policy.

4. Financing a major war is virtually certain to provoke inflation. Fiscal techniques are now much more sophisticated than they were at the time of World War I, not to mention earlier wars, but all-out war involves mobilizing such a large part of total output that even the best known financial techniques can not cover the cost from taxes and voluntary loans.

5. The transition from war to peace may be as inflation-prone as the transition from peace to war.

6. The public will continue to use an established money long after its purchasing power is seen to be declining at a substantial rate. At some not-precisely-predictable rate of decline, however, they may completely lose confidence in it and try to spend it as soon as they receive it; perhaps this will occur when its purchasing power declines appreciably between one payday and the next. In such circumstances you try to get your debtors to pay you at once, you try to hold off your creditors as long as possible, you press your employers for shorter and shorter pay periods, and you buy up physical objects of any kind that is available with any money you can not spend at once. This is hyperinflation or runaway inflation: the velocity of circulation rises sharply and may outdo the increase in the money supply in generating the rise in prices.

Chapter 3

THE ROLE OF MONEY IN INFLATION

The Demand-Pull Explanation

For over 400 years the standard explanation of inflation has been an excessive increase in the supply of money,* or "too much money chasing too few goods", in the catchy phrase popularized since World War II. This has come to be known as "demand-pull" inflation, in contrast to the "cost-push" explanation that gained credence in the 1950's and after. It is clearly rooted in the quantity theory of money and prices ("the quantity theory" for short), in the context of a schematic representation of the economy known as the "model" of pure competition, both of which are summarized in the Appendix.

The model assumes that there are many sellers and many buyers of each particular product, and no seller or buyer has significant market power or has any reason to prefer any buyer or seller over any other. In effect, all transactions take place in auction markets; prices are flexible, hence all markets "clear" (supply and demand will be in balance). Workers offer their labour in one market, up to the point at which they prefer to enjoy more leisure instead of more consumption. Owners of productive property offer the services of their land, buildings, and machinery in other markets. Entrepreneurs buy the services of these "factors of production", as they are called, and use them to produce goods and services for sale to consumers; they hope to make a "pure" profit, i.e. to earn more than the mere wages of management, by finding more cost-efficient methods of production. Workers, owners of capital goods, and entrepreneurs thus earn income in the process of production, which they then spend in consumer markets to buy the products they have helped to make.

Competitive forces in this model ensure that the economy's resources are used most efficiently for the satisfaction of human wants—or at least that they **tend** to be so used in the long run. Involuntary unemployment and other imbalances may occur temporarily, but in the end everyone earns the going wage for his particular skills and has no more or no less

---

*There are many possible definitions of money, and economists are by no means agreed as to which is best or whether the same definition is appropriate in all cases. For the purposes of the quantity theory of money and prices, and therefore for the purposes of this chapter, it should be interpreted as meaning those and only those things that can be used to effect transactions without first being exchanged for something else. In most jurisdictions this means coins, banknotes or currency-notes, and chequeable deposits.

work than he wants. Competitive forces also ensure—or tend to ensure—that the benefits of technical progress are passed on to the general public in the form of lower prices. In principle the system could work on a barter basis, but the use of money makes it work more efficiently. The amount of money available to the economy is taken as given at any particular time, and the general price level is determined by the quantity theory of money and prices. Obviously, then, inflation will occur if and only if the money supply grows more rapidly than the flow of goods and services the economy is able to produce.

Of course, the markets postulated in this model have little resemblance to those in which you and I sell our services and make our purchases. Only organized markets in certain commodities or in securities can claim to approximate auction markets, and even there trading is usually dominated by a few relatively-large-scale operators. The model is deficient in other respects too, as we will point out later in this chapter, yet it is the philosophical basis for much of the mythology of the free-enterprise profit-motivated system. Indeed, until the 1930's no better model was available to economists as a framework for policy recommendations. Despite its shortcomings, however, the model does provide a useful starting-point for understanding a money-and-market economy. Also, it is helpful in drawing policy conclusions for the real world, provided sufficient allowances are made for its deficiencies; unfortunately, this has not always been done.

The Monetarist Explanation

You may already be familiar with the monetarist school of thought, which is dominated by Milton Friedman, and the long controversy between its adherents and Keynesian economists (followers of the late J.M. Keynes). For our present purposes the main points to note are four: (1) Though monetarists usually emphasize their links with the quantity theory of an earlier day, monetarism is not primarily a theory of the general price level; it deals in a much broader way with the part money plays in the economy. (2) Despite monetarist emphasis on the role of money, which gives them their name, their disputes with Keynesians are not really about money as such but about the analytical framework from which they derive their conclusions. (3) Friedman and most other monetarists are advocates of a rather extreme version of *laissez faire* economic policies. (4) Monetarists explicitly reject most of Keynesian economics (explained more fully in Chapter 7 and in section 6 of the Appendix), which offers an explanation of chronic unemployment and advocates certain corrective policies.

Monetarists have made important contributions to our understanding not only of the role of money in the economy but also of many other aspects of economic activity. Not the least of their contributions has been in helping to debunk some of the more extreme positions taken by some professing Keynesians. A brief summary of their views will be found in section 7 of the Appendix, and they will also enter the discussion in Chapters 7 and 10. If you want to pursue their ideas in greater detail, you should consult Friedman's own writings and those of other monetarists.[1]

The monetarist position on inflation is that it is always and everywhere a monetary phenomenon, in the sense that it is and can be produced only by a more rapid increase in the quantity of money than in output. It follows that the cure is simple: reduce the money supply as quickly as possible (it is not clear how rapidly monetarists think this could be done in practice), then allow it to increase at a moderate but stable rate, say 3 to 5 percent a year, to accommodate the growth of real output.

What would this do to unemployment? Well, here Friedman's *laissez-faire* predilections come to the fore. He believes there is a "natural" rate of unemployment, consistent with equilibrium in the structure of real wages, below which monetary policy can not peg the unemployment rate for long. He denies the existence of **involuntary** unemployment, attributes the observed ("voluntary") unemployment to government policies that make leisure more attractive than work or to imperfect information and errors in decisionmaking, and argues that bringing the money supply (and therefore inflation) under control would substantially reduce unemployment. He is opposed to the use of fiscal measures to support the spending stream, and in fact would like to reduce the economic role of government to a minimum.

"Cost-Push" and "Inflationary Expectations"

By the early 1950's some economists began to identify what they considered a new kind of inflation, cost-push inflation, and to contrast it with "old-fashioned" demand-pull inflation. Their arguments have considerable plausibility, since increasing prices of raw materials, labour, intermediate goods, and other inputs do mean rising costs to any producer, which he will naturally try to pass on in his selling prices. Any price increase in an inflationary environment, even one that is in itself merely functional, appears to be an inflationary increase in costs to those who must pay it, and is thus in part the cause of more inflation.

However, cost-push offers no explanation of why a given producer's costs (i.e. his suppliers' selling prices) are rising in the first place, nor where the buyer gets the money from to pay continually higher prices for his purchases. Nor is this a new phenomenon; costs have always pushed against prices, and the very essence of a profit-motivated economic system is the incentive to outmanoeuvre these pressures by adaptations or innovations of some kind. Why is it that cost pressures sometimes succeed in raising prices, sometimes fail, and sometimes are more than offset by deflationary pressures? Thus, though the distinction between demand-pull and cost-push forces is certainly helpful, it does not get us much farther forward; in particular, since it is not really a new phenomenon, it can not justify the assertion that today's inflation is categorically different from the inflations of the past.

Another thesis that has been advanced is that inflationary expectations become self-fulfilling and ensure that further inflation will occur. There is indeed a great deal of truth in this observation, but it should be ascribed to the **recognition**, not the anticipation, of inflation. Once people come to realize that prices are rising and that there is little they as individuals can do to stop the process, that realization will weaken their resistance to further price increases and will therefore make it easier for the cost-push process to continue. At most, however, this is a supplementary factor that speeds up the process; it does not explain what starts the inflation that people eventually come to recognize, nor where the money comes from to finance the ever-increasing rate of spending.

Big Government, Big Labour, Big Business

Three other explanations often offered for inflation may be treated together, because they are essentially similar except that the identity of the alleged villain differs: (1) inflation is caused by excessive government spending and budgetary deficits; (2) inflation is caused by unrealistic wage demands by powerful trade unions; (3) inflation is caused by the excessive profits business seeks to obtain or is able to command by reason of its market power. Business leaders blame the government and labour; politicians blame labour and business; labour leaders blame the government and business. Could it be that they are all two-thirds right?

Unquestionably, unwise or selfish actions in any of these three sectors would generate or add to cost-push pressures in the economy. By the same token, the real incomes of all other members of the community would fare better in an inflationary environment if any important sector were to passively accept reductions in its real income. But a money-and-market economy does not work that way: it is based on the premise that everyone is entitled to improve his real income by making the best deal he can in the market. The money-and-market system is not divinely ordained and is far from perfect, but under proper constraints it offers the ordinary citizen a better prospect than known alternatives. In any case, however, blaming inflation on the greed of others (not **us**, of course!) leaves unanswered the question of where the public finds the money income with which to pay the prices demanded.

It is certainly true that unwise or improvident government policies can generate inflation, but deficits are not necessarily unwise or improvident. Indeed, the significance of government deficits is widely misunderstood, because common government accounting practices differ in important ways from private accounting practices. Many government financial statements treat capital expenditures the same as current expenditures, i.e. they write them off entirely in the year they are made, instead of charging only depreciation or other capital-cost allowances— for the very good reason that this minimizes the possibility of creating fictitious surpluses (or concealing true deficits) by understating depreciation. To the extent that government deficit-financing can be linked to useful capital projects, therefore, it is in the same category as private deficit-financing (borrowing) for capital purposes. Furthermore, deficits in excess of capital spending may be fully justified if there is no better way of supporting an appropriate level of economic activity. And tax-financed expenditures for social-insurance and similar purposes ("transfer payments"), while they may indeed reduce the real incomes of taxpayers and may indeed weaken the work-incentives of some recipients, also meet real needs; provided they are soundly based and economically administered, they reflect the community's judgment about how its total real income should be shared, and must therefore be respected.

Wage and salary increases in excess of improvements in the general productivity of the economy certainly do add to inflationary pressures, but the same is true of increases in interest, dividends, rents, and other returns to the owners of property. Obviously, the increase in total money income (which boils down to wages and salaries or their equivalent plus returns to property) must be limited to the increase in real output if inflation is to be avoided. This is not an easy problem to solve in a free economy (and even the centrally-planned economies seem to be having very similar problems), but it is greatly complicated by the fact that its solution also involves deciding how the community's real income is to be divided—not only how it is to be divided between "labour" and "capital", but also how it is to be divided among various categories of wage- and salary-earners and among the various categories of investors who own or finance the community's capital stock. We will meet some of these complications in Chapters 8 and 11.

The role of profits in a money-and-market system is often misunderstood, even by those who feel most constrained to defend them. In part this is due to some confusion over terminology. "Profit" is often used in a broad sense to include all returns on invested capital, and even the emoluments of management, whereas in the sense of the motivating force in the market system it has a much narrower meaning. Capital must earn a reasonable profit in the broad sense (i.e. in the form of interest, dividends, rents, etc.) in order to encourage savers to put their savings to productive use, otherwise the economy's productive capacity and real income would be much lower. But, what is a "reasonable" return? Even when quite low average rates of return (compared to past experience) obtain over a considerable period, it does not necessarily follow that the community as a whole will begin to consume its capital; the only clear criterion is that the rate of return in any particular type of business must not fall persistently below the average rate in other types of business, or its capital equipment will not be renewed when it wears out.

In the sense that is relevant for understanding "the profit motive", however, the word has a much narrower meaning, as noted at the start of this chapter: a "true" or "pure" profit over and above normal returns to capital and management. In a fully competitive economy the **hope** of winning a profit in this sense is the carrot that induces the private-enterprise horse to pull the cart of economic progress; it need not be large, and it should always tend to disappear as competitors identify and apply the new techniques for their own use. (See also section 2 of the Appendix.)

All three of these "explanations" of inflation really deal primarily with the size of the economy's real income and how it is divided up among the populace, not with how inflation is generated. Wage-and-salary bargaining determines both the money wages of individual workers and the overall distribution of money incomes between labour and capital; if one person or group gets more real income as a result, others get less. Should strikes or lockouts occur in the course of negotiations, the real output (real income) of the community suffers accordingly and there is less of it to divide up. Government taxes to finance wanted community services are equivalent to the money paid to the private sector for the products they provide us with. Taxes paid to finance transfer payments reflect the community's decisions on how its real income should be shared, as already noted. Government spending financed by borrowing, if soundly based, either finances useful capital projects or helps to prevent unemployment and to support the economy's real income. **Wasteful** spending anywhere in the economy—whether in the private or the government sector—reduces the real income available for distribution, but it does not explain how inflation arises.

Weak Theoretical Foundations

All the "explanations" of inflation so far discussed are based on very shaky foundations. The cost-push, expectations, big-government, big-labour, and big-business explanations are particularly weak in that they offer no account of where the public gets the increased money income needed to buy the same real output at ever-increasing prices. Friedman, on the other hand, is very explicit on this point: it can come only from a disproportionate increase in the money supply. The demand-pull explanation is just as specific—it must come from either an increase in the money supply or an increase in its velocity of circulation (which Friedman believes is normally quite stable). Even though they fail to say so explicitly, however, we must conclude that the other five explanations also rely on an increase in the money supply or in its velocity as an integral part of the process, since there is no other possible way in which money income could expand.* It follows that at most they supplement the quantity-theory explanation of inflation, they do not supplant it.

In all seven of these explanations, therefore, money is the real villain. How is it, then, that the authorities allow the money supply to expand unduly? Surely they, too, know all about the quantity theory. Only the monetarists acknowledge this question and offer an answer: they say it is due to misinformation on someone's part, or mistaken official policies (perhaps undertaken with good intentions), or both.

However, it is not really the quantity theory as such that is open to question, but the broad theoretical framework behind the analysis. Both the demand-pull and the monetarist explanations are based on models of pure competition that are admittedly much more sophisticated than the simple version briefly described in the opening section of this chapter and in section 2 of the Appendix, but that do not differ materially in their basic assumptions and therefore arrive at essentially the same conclusions. The other five explanations are not as clearly identifiable with the

---

* It is of course true that an inflationary price rise could occur in one period with the same money income as in the preceding period, or even a reduced one, if there were a decline in real output (or in the physical volume of transactions to be effected with money); in fact that has actually happened occasionally in more than one country in recent years, not to mention the 1930's. In fairness, however, we must note that all seven explanations either talk in terms of a given level of real output or explicitly deny that output can falter (except perhaps as a temporary disturbance).

model of pure competition, but are much influenced by it, since it still underlies most formal instruction in economics and since the proponents of these explanations seem to accept most of its conclusions. In some cases they uncritically invoke the long-run-equilibrium* implications of the model in order to derive current policy conclusions. In other cases they employ truncated versions of the process by which the model says long-run equilibrium is attained in the face of a short-run disturbance or departure from equilibrium, thus implying that the equilibrating process is very rapid if not virtually instantaneous.

The ignoring or truncating of the equilibrating process is particularly surprising in the case of the monetarists, who pride themselves on the continuity of their analysis with the older versions of the quantity theory. Irving Fisher, the father of the main North American version of the quantity theory, placed great stress on the difference between "periods of transition" (in which he acknowledged his theory was not rigidly true, but equilibrating forces were at work) and "periods of equilibrium" (in which he believed his theory fully applied). He noted that transition periods lasted until old contracts expired and were renegotiated, hence were apt to be quite long. Furthermore he noted that one transition period might merge into a succession of subsequent transition periods, as new short-run disturbances occurred. At one point he said, "Since periods of transition are the rule and those of equilibrium the exception, the mechanism of exchange is almost always in a dynamic rather than a static condition."[2]

We have already noted that the model of pure competition postulates markets that bear little resemblance to those you and I know. Also, it ignores many important characteristics of real-world economies: the rise and importance of labour unions; the evolution of industry from the putting-out system of Adam Smith's day to the factory system, to large multiproduct firms, and to modern multinational corporations; industrial concentration; changes in technology; the rise of the service industries; changes in laws, institutions, customs, ideologies, and social values; and other factors that affect human behavior in the economic sphere. In the 1930's the model of imperfect or monopolistic competition was introduced, which materially modifies the assumptions and therefore the conclusions of the older model (see section 5 of the Appendix). It offers explanations of such things as branded products, advertizing and selling costs, markets in which there are relatively few

---

* Long-run equilibrium means a situation in which normal market forces have had time to correct all short-run imbalances in all markets, so there is no incentive to change the allocation of resources among firms or industries. See also sections 2 and 3 of the Appendix.

buyers or few sellers, and other things the older model could not account for, but monetarists and their allies make no use of it whatever.* Even the new model of competition is far from perfect, however; further study of how prices are actually set in the real world is badly needed, as is argued in Chapter 6.

The critical points here are (1) these explanations of inflation do not make effective use of the available theoretical material about how the economy operates, and (2) they do not acknowledge the shortcomings of the models they do use, nor make allowances for these shortcomings when making policy recommendations. It follows that their analytical conclusions must be heavily discounted for any application in the world of reality.

Historical Evidence

Any inflation is clearly a monetary phenomenon, in the sense that a disproportionate increase in the money supply is a necessary condition. It is also clear that an injection of an excessive amount of money in any economy is sufficient to generate an inflation. But the fact that it is both a necessary and a sufficient condition does not mean that "excessive monetary expansion" is always an adequate explanation of the causes of inflation. Even a cursory review of historical examples shows that non-monetary factors have played an important role in most if not all cases.

An expansion of the money supply at a more rapid rate than output may fairly be identified as the **immediate cause** of many inflations. However, causal sequences in human affairs are seldom simple or clear-cut; behind most immediate causes there lie complex concatenations of circumstances and relationships, among which it may be virtually impossible to identify any single ultimate cause. Thus the sudden inflow of large quantities of gold and silver from the Western Hemisphere in the 16th century, as described in Chapter 2, was clearly the immediate cause of the subsequent inflation in Europe. Even here, however, this apparently-external "disturbance" to the system becomes the result of other elements of the system if we widen our horizon to include the historical sequences of exploration and conquest that lay behind it.

Much the same is true of the more-spectacular inflations associated with paper currencies. In some cases the overissue of money was clearly

---

* It must be admitted, however, that the monetarists and their allies are not by any means alone in this respect. The economics profession in general has made disappointingly little progress at integrating the new model into the main body of economic theory; even advanced textbooks still rely heavily on models that do not improve very much on the simpler versions of the model of pure competition.

the immediate cause, perhaps triggered by simple mismanagement or by inadequate control over the credit-expanding potential of paper money, but the causal sequence leads back to the social, economic, and political climate in which these events occurred. In other cases the overissue was a deliberate choice by the monetary authorities as the lesser of the two evils: the classic examples are to be found in war finance even as recently as World War II, as noted in the third section of Chapter 2.

In still other cases it is not even clear that excessive monetary expansion can be said to have been the immediate cause of inflation. Look back at the description of the German inflation after World War I, in Chapter 2. Would you care to identify "the" cause? Was it a simple case of the overissue of money? Was it the continuing deficits of a weak government? Was it the too-vigorous pursuit of social reform by the German public, preventing the government from following a more restrictive fiscal policy? Was it the Carthaginian peace treaty, against which the late J.M. Keynes had inveighed so eloquently already?[3] Was it the intransigeance of France and Belgium and their occupation of the Ruhr?

A convinced exponent of the quantity theory might indeed say that "allowing" the money supply to increase inordinately was "the" cause of the inflation, but surely that would be making a Procrustean bed of the theory and forcing the facts to fit it. The assumptions on which the theory rests did not obtain: prices were **not** passive, but were strongly influenced by "real" (nonmonetary) economic forces and in turn put pressure on the fiscal authorities to expand the money supply; the increase in the money supply did not occur as an independent disturbance from "outside" the system, but as a response by the government to a Hobson's-Choice situation. No doubt the rising money supply did generate further pressure towards rising prices, but a chain of causation also linked reparations payments to price increases and thence to increases in the money supply. It is by no means clear whether the chain of causation ran more strongly from money to prices or from prices to money. Economic theory then had only rather unsophisticated versions of the quantity theory of money and prices to rely on, yet reputable contemporary economists concluded that the causal sequence ran from exchange-rate depreciation to increasing domestic prices and wages to increasing public demand for cash and increasing government deficits and then to monetary expansion.

Unquestionably an excessive increase in the money supply was a necessary condition for the German inflation. Unquestionably, also, wiser policies at home and abroad might well have avoided the hyperinflation; but, given the magnitude of the reparations demanded, some degree of inflation could hardly have been avoided even if France and Belgium had refrained from occupying the Ruhr. The reparations burden, onerous in amount and abruptly imposed, does stand out as a major factor, but a substantial and persistent inflation was already under way when the Reparations Commission reported. Surely the only reasonable conclusion is that there was no single cause, but a complex set of interacting causal forces and circumstances.

The Validation Thesis

One conclusion that emerges from all this is that an expansion of the money supply at a rate materially in excess of the community's real output is a necessary condition for inflation to develop,* but nonmonetary factors may (and usually do) play an important role as well.

A second conclusion is that what is sometimes known as "the validation thesis" seems to offer a much more persuasive explanation of the role of money in the almost-world-wide inflation that exists today. It is compatible with Keynesian and other nonmonetarist thought, and it may also prove acceptable to some monetarists, for it would require merely a modification of their views on the causal role of money rather than a complete about-face. (It will do nothing to reduce monetarist and nonmonetarist disputes over economic policies, however, since they stem from categorically-different analytical assumptions.)

There are two main elements in the validation thesis. First, it accepts markets and marketing procedures as they are found in reality, or models that give the best available approximation of reality, instead of the auction-type markets of pure competition. They may be thought of in terms of the model of imperfect or monopolistic competition; or, better still, with the addition of the features described in Chapters 5 and 6. Sellers may be expected to set whatever asking prices they believe will give them maximum net returns within a reasonable time horizon, whether they are selling their own labour or a professional service or some physical product; in general they will be biased in favour of higher prices, limited primarily by the fact that too high a price will drive trade to other sellers or to other products and leave them with an excessive inventory of unsold goods and a smaller net income. Buyers in strong bargaining positions may set offering prices that are biased towards the low end of their market expectations, but the average consumer will

---

* The only significant exception is a sudden major increase in the velocity of circulation of money, as when people become completely disenchanted with their currency and try desperately to get rid of it; but this is only likely to happen in the advanced stages of a severe inflation, when it turns into the rare phase known as hyperinflation.

have little choice but to accept the best deal that he can find or do without. For the economy as a whole, excessive asking prices spell reduced output (i.e. reduced real income) and more unemployment.

The second element of the validation thesis is the fact that virtually all governments nowadays are committed to supporting a high level of output and employment, even though this support is badly compromised at present by efforts to restrain inflation. (We will argue later that these anti-inflation policies are misguided and ineffective, but that is irrelevant here.) In the old days the economy's money income was essentially a zero-sum game, as explained in the third section of Chapter 7: if someone got more, someone else got less, because the spending stream was limited by an inflexible money supply. It was a far-from-perfect boom-and-bust system, but there was no systematic bias towards inflation; prices sometimes rose for a while, but sometimes fell, and the probabilities were about equal. Now, however, the situation is materially changed. If potential real output valued at current asking prices is significantly greater than the spending stream can accommodate, and unemployment of human and material resources therefore rises above some critical level, the authorities can be counted on to initiate fiscal or monetary measures that will raise the spending stream enough to make good at least a part of the deficiency. That means that a significant part of the price increases sellers are asking will be **validated** by an increase in the money supply and in money income. The authorities are fully aware that allowing the money supply to increase will release inflationary pressures, but not doing so will mean that some part of potential output will go unrealized (or that the unrealized potential already in evidence will increase) and unemployment will worsen. **That** is what makes today's inflation categorically different from those of the past.

Chapter 4
EXTERNAL ASPECTS

Imported Inflation

Most countries can claim, with some show of reason, that a substantial part of their inflations is imported from abroad. This is particularly true of small and medium-sized countries that earn a substantial part of their incomes from external trade and rely on imports to supply much of their day-to-day needs. However, we will argue in the second section of Chapter 7 that The Fearsome Dilemma is essentially a domestic problem; if it can be solved satisfactorily at that level, especially by the major powers, then the world's balance-of-payments problems should prove relatively easy to resolve. If international monetary arrangements are a subject you are not prepared to spend much time or effort in penetrating, therefore, you will not lose the thread of the discussion if you skip this chapter and pass on directly to the next. Nevertheless it remains true that we live in an interdependent world, and even the most powerful nations can not entirely neglect either the effects of their actions on other nations or the reciprocal effects of events and policies abroad on their own economies. By skipping this chapter you will be ignoring a number of important considerations that must be taken into account in judging the implications of a given set of domestic policies.

All countries, even the most nearly self-sufficient in resources, depend on imports for certain key supplies and services. Inflation abroad means rising costs of these imports, unless promptly offset by a favourable change in the exchange rate, and means that domestic producers of competing goods can demand higher prices too. By itself this would be deflationary in any given country and would reduce real income, because the same domestic money income could not cover the old volume of imports at the new higher prices and the old volume of domestic goods at the old prices; probably imports and domestic output would both weaken. However, inflation abroad also means that the country's exports will fetch increasing prices in world markets, which means higher incomes for domestic producers and leads to more spending, so in this case at least we can identify where some of the money comes from to support the domestic spending stream. Exporters will spend most of their added receipts on some combination of imports and domestic goods, so the total volume of imports may fall very little if at all, and (if the price of exports rises more than that of imports) real income may actually increase. Higher export earnings also mean an increase in the country's external reserves, which will encourage domestic monetary expansion.

The sharp increase in oil prices on world markets in the 1970's may be cited as a special case of imported inflation by oil importers.* Some critics blame the Organization of Petroleum Exporting Countries (OPEC) for most, perhaps all, of the great upsurge in world inflation that followed. Well, as we have already noted, **any** price increase appears inflationary to those who have to pay it, in the sense that they must either pass it on in their own selling prices or lose an equivalent amount of real income. For their part the oil producers claimed they were simply acting defensively, to protect themselves against the rising prices of what they buy. Aside from the fact that their cartel is more openly acknowledged and perhaps more successful than some others, are they really acting any differently than the producers of other products? Does General Motors set the prices of its automobiles on world markets with a compassionate eye on the "need" for transportation at home and abroad? Should OPEC be more considerate of the "needs" of other countries for energy than those countries are of OPEC's "needs" for imports?

Imported inflation in this simple sense thus seems able to explain how any one country can get the money to support an expansion of its spending stream, but how about the world as a whole? If one country gets an inflationary inflow of money in this way, won't there be a corresponding **deflation** in the country that loses the money?

Well, that is pretty much what happened in the days when the gold standard was generally adhered to in most major countries. Gold was the basic form of international money, i.e. it was the form in which international payments had to be settled if any question arose. Furthermore each individual country maintained a fairly definite ratio between its gold reserves and its domestic money supply. The result was that if one country gained gold its money supply tended to increase by some multiple of that gain, and if another lost gold its money supply tended to contract by some multiple of that loss, with corresponding effects on their spending streams. However, all this has now changed. The world's supply of external reserves is no longer constrained by the need to maintain convertibility into gold. Exchange rates are no longer fixed, they are flexible. There is no longer an effective link between a country's external reserves and its domestic money supply. Imported inflation in one country no longer implies deflation elsewhere.

---

* In this case, of course, there was no corresponding increase in export earnings by the oil importers; the addition to the domestic spending stream came from expansionary domestic measures to finance the additional import bill.

External Reserves

All countries keep external reserves in one form or another, as they have done since time immemorial. They have two major functions: to defend the exchange rate of the currency when that is deemed appropriate, and to give assured access to essential imports in time of need. Under the full gold standard, when residents as well as nonresidents had the right (in principle at least) to convert domestic paper money into gold coin, what we now call external reserves were also domestic reserves; they ensured convertibility, and thereby limited the domestic money supply. In the last 50 years or so, however, there have been important changes in their perceived roles.

First, the relative importance of the two major roles of external reserves has changed. Defending the exchange rate was seen as the main function in gold-standard days; reserves are still so used, but that function does not get nearly as high a priority as it used to. (In fact there are wide differences of opinion about how flexible the exchange rate should be, but we needn't get involved in that debate; the essential point for our purposes is simply that the international community is now much more permissive about exchange-rate policies.) The precautionary function, assurance of access to essential imports in time of need, has always been an important reason for holding external reserves, but it was seen as secondary under gold-standard conditions; nowadays many people consider it the main function.

The second important change relates to the relationship between a country's external reserves and its domestic money supply. Convertibility into gold or the equivalent used to be thought necessary to maintain confidence in the currency, and as already noted that put a limit (flexible but finite) on it. However, this link was effectively broken many years ago in most countries, for reasons to be noted shortly. The U.S.A. was the last holdout; it maintained effective convertibility until the 1950's, and nominal convertibility until 1971. Reserves are now to be used as the national interests dictate, and may be reduced to zero (or even below zero, in the sense that the authorities may borrow abroad to replenish them) for good reasons.

Third, gold is a much smaller part of external reserves for most countries and for the world as a whole than it was in the heyday of the gold standard before 1914, or even what it was just before the U.S.A. severed the last vestige of dollar-convertibility in 1971, and its role is very different. At the official International Monetary Fund (the I.M.F. or the Fund) valuation it is now substantially less than 10 percent of total world reserves. As recently as the end of 1969 it was almost exactly 50

Composition of World Reserves at Selected Dates
(Billions of Special Drawing Rights*)

Reserve Category	End of: 1937	1948	1959	1969	1972	1978	1983
Gold @ SDR35.00 per oz.	25.3	32.8	37.9	39.1	35.8	36.3	33.1
Foreign exchange	2.3	13.5	16.2	32.4	95.4	224.2	317.3
Fund reserve positions†	—	1.6	3.3	6.7	6.3	14.8	39.1
Special Drawing Rights	—	—	—	—	8.7	8.1	14.4
Grand total	27.6	47.8	57.4	78.3	146.2	283.4	403.9
Memorandum:							
Use of Fund credit	—	0.2	0.4	4.0	1.1	10.3	30.0

Source: International Monetary Fund, *International Financial Statistics*, various
issues.

* The Special Drawing Right was equivalent to US$1.00000 until December
1971, US$1.08571 from then until January 1973, and US$1.20635 from
February 1973 to June 1974. Thereafter the equivalent is computed from a
weighted average of rates for a specified list of major currencies; it was
US$1.30279 at the end of 1978, and US$1.10311 at the end of 1983. Its highest
value to date was US$1.34939 (or the lowest value of the dollar was
SDR0.741074) on 30th October 1978.

† Members' reserve-tranche positions plus lendings to the Fund.

---

percent, and a decade earlier it was 66 percent; see the table on this page.
Of course its market price has recently fluctuated between roughly ten
and twenty times its official value, which would again make it 50 percent
or more of the total. However, gold is really just another commodity
now, and a commodity with a very volatile price; nations are clearly
reluctant to use it for settling trade balances, and prefer to either hold on
to it for further speculative gains or sell it off in the world bullion
market. One may question the propriety of still counting it as an
international money at all.

A new and relatively small, but growing, part of international reserves
now consists of the credit facilities of the Fund, partly in the form of
loans of other countries' currencies made available through a system of
subscriptions and quotas and partly in a more complex form called
Special Drawing Rights (SDR's). In principle the Fund may eventually be
able to regulate the supply of international reserves to its members in
much the same way as a national central bank regulates the supply of

reserves to domestic commercial banks (and thereby regulates the money supply, as explained in the next section of this chapter). In practice, however this is pretty hard to do satisfactorily by an international committee, and at present it is impossible because there are other ways of generating internationally-acceptable reserves.

By far the largest part of international reserves today consists of the national currencies of certain countries (generally known as "key currencies") that are used as international monies not only by other countries but also by their residents; the total supply of these reserves is entirely outside the control of the Fund. The table shows that the total, now mostly U.S. dollars, was SDR16-billion at the end of 1959, SDR32-billion at the end of 1969, and SDR317-billion at the end of 1983—or US$16-billion, US$32-billion, and US$350-billion respectively.

Parkinson's Law of Reserves

You are probably familiar with at least the main essentials of what may be called "the fractional-reserve principle" as it applies to the domestic banking system of your own national economy; it can be shown that there are important parallels in international monetary affairs. A simple illustration of how it works at the national level can easily be put together, if we ignore the fact that some domestic spending "leaks away" to pay for imports. (The main effect of the leakage is to reduce the multiple expansion we are about to look at; it is especially important for small countries).

Most countries have a central bank like the Federal Reserve System in the U.S.A., the Bank of England, or the Bank of France, which issues banknotes and accepts deposits from commercial banks. Now let us suppose this central bank buys some gold or foreign exchange or domestic securities or whatever it thinks wise, and pays for its purchase by issuing $1000 (or one thousand pounds or marks or francs or whatever is the local money), and let us suppose further that the public likes to keep 10 percent of its money in cash and 90 percent in chequeing deposits. That means that $900 of the newly-issued $1000 will soon be deposited in various commercial banks, which can now lend some portion of these deposits but must keep a certain fraction of them on deposit with the central bank as a reserve—this being the derivation of the term "fractional-reserve principle".

A process of expansion begins by a sequence of loans and redeposits, which will raise the total increase in the money supply to $5,263 if the reserve-ratio kept by the commercial banks is 10 percent, and $3,571 if the ratio is 20 percent. In the first case the central bank's new obligations become $526 in notes held by the public and $474 in commercial-bank reserves, just enough to support the public's new deposits of $4,737, and the total increase in the money supply is $526 + $4,737 = $5,263; in the second case the figures become $357, $643, $3,214, and $357 + $3,214 = $3,571 respectively. You might call this Parkinson's Law of Reserves: the money supply expands to absorb the available reserves.

Now for the international application. External reserves are the fractional-reserve medium for central banks, and Parkinson's Law of Reserves operates there too: a central bank's monetary obligations tend to expand until they absorb the available external reserves, just as the domestic money supply tends to expand till it absorbs the reserves the central bank provides to the commercial banks. (Hence the domestic money supply increases by a double multiple of any increase in external reserves.) In the old days gold-convertibility did put some limits on the potential expansion, as already noted, as long as all countries did not inflate simultaneously. Nowadays an increase in external reserves still implies an expansion of the money supply (and therefore of the spending stream as well), and a decrease implies a contraction, but the central bank may choose to override either effect if it appears that the national interest so requires. Because of The Fearsome Dilemma, however, it is more likely to override a loss of reserves (which would tend to increase unemployment, probably already high) than to override an increase (which implies that spending will increase and unemployment will be reduced).

The Key-Currency System

The practice of holding external reserves in the form of selected national currencies instead of or as well as gold goes a long way back in history, and arose out of the practical decisions of practical men, not any explicit international agreement; it was simply an extension of the standard practice of foreign traders and their bankers, who from time immemorial have held working balances in foreign currencies. Since the precautionary function of reserves has always been of major importance, ready convertibility into a wide range of goods and services at relatively stable prices is a requirement of a good reserve medium. Gold met this test admirably when most currencies were pegged to it at fixed exchange rates, but the national currency of another nation may also serve the purpose very well, especially if the issuing country's industries produce a wide range of goods and services at prices that are competitive on world markets, and if it has a strong financial system with good markets in which traders can employ their temporarily-idle funds or finance their capital needs. Such a currency is, or has the potential of becoming, a key currency.

Between 1870 and 1914 dual gold-and-silver or bimetallic standards were generally abandoned in favour of the gold standard. This meant a considerable increase in the demand for gold either as standard gold coin in circulation or (more commonly) as reserves, whereas the supply of monetary gold was increasing more slowly than world trade or world income. The problem was eased to some extent by the withdrawal of gold coin from circulation into national reserves, and its replacement by paper currency or chequeable deposits that were in principle convertible into gold on demand, but even so the world's gold reserves had to be stretched ever thinner to avoid deflation. In this context the gold-exchange standard gained ready acceptance: all or a major part of the nation's external reserves might be held as balances denominated in another currency that was directly convertible into gold. For a country newly assuming the responsibilities of the gold standard this arrangement avoided the need to acquire a substantial initial stock of gold; it avoided the costs of holding, protecting, and shipping gold; and it meant that the reserves could be invested in securities denominated in the reserve currency, thus earning an appreciable interest return. (Of course there were disadvantages, too, including the risk that the reserve currency might some day be devalued, though that probably seemed a remote possibility for holders of sterling before World War I.) Sterling was the leading world currency and was widely used in world trade, not only with or through Britain and British dependencies but also between other sovereign countries; in short it was the major key currency of that day, although the term was not then in use, so it was a logical choice as a reserve medium.

Furthermore it must be recognized that the gold-exchange standard constituted a material advance in international arrangements, in that it introduced much-needed elasticity into the system. The supply of gold is inelastic, and in times of crisis the whole financial system (domestic or international or both) would freeze up if everyone tried to convert his assets into gold at once. This sort of thing need not happen with reserves denominated in a well-managed key currency, for the issuing central bank can deal with domestic financial panics by exercising its lender-of-last-resort function, and the demand for reserves by other countries is small compared to the domestic demand for the key currency.

Paradoxically enough, the real growth of the use of national currencies as international-reserve media came after the collapse of the gold standard. Britain ended the convertibility of its currency into gold in 1931, as did most other countries except the U.S.A. about the same time, but the link to gold proved irrelevant. Countries with currencies tied to sterling found it continued to give them most of the same benefits as before; they evolved into the sterling area, which enjoyed a substantial multilateral freedom of trade and capital movements among its members in a world of exchange controls and other problems. A somewhat similar but smaller group formed around the French franc, and a large but less-formal group linked itself to the U.S. dollar. World War II and its aftermath largely undermined the British and the French systems, and by the late 1950's creeping inflation put the dollar under pressure as well, though nominal convertibility into gold was maintained until 1971. Thus the gold-exchange standard became the key-currency standard.

Key Currencies and Inflation

A key-currency system works quite well as long as the issuing country's exports remain competitive on world markets—the practice would never have become so firmly established if this were not so. It works well in that case because the key currency is in effect readily convertible into goods and services in the markets of the issuing country, so no-one (neither the monetary authorities of another country nor any person resident there) need hold any more of it than he finds convenient for his own transactions or precautionary needs; and residents of third countries will willingly accept it in settlement of accounts, because they can use it in the same way or convert it into key-currency-country exports at will.

When the exports of the key-currency country become less-than-fully competitive in world markets, however, the situation changes dramatically. Once accepted as an international money, a currency will long continue to be so used even when its usefulness is clearly declining—for exactly the same reasons that domestic money continues to be used into the last stages of hyperinflation. In effect, the key-currency country is able to buy imports with its own IOU's (claims on its domestic banking system) even though it no longer tries or is no longer able to maintain convertibility into other currencies at fixed exchange rates.

In any country that is not a key-currency country, a major constraint on both public and private spending is the fact that much of it will spill over into demand for imports, regardless of whether the spending is wasteful and extravagant or part of a well-planned program of economic development or anything in between. A country whose external reserves are declining is either overconsuming (i.e. consuming more imports than it is currently earning through exports) or else spending more on capital formation than it can finance out of domestic saving plus net borrowing abroad; perhaps both. It may be perfectly justified in doing so—its overspending may be for temporary food imports because of a domestic crop failure, its capital spending program may be entirely sound. That is not the point. The point is that domestic spending is ultimately limited by external reserves and external borrowing, regardless of whether the spending is good, bad, or indifferent in itself. An increase in external reserves above some minimum prudent level is therefore a signal to the domestic authorities that they may permit more spending in the domestic economy; this may add somewhat to inflationary pressures at home, but much of it will go on imports, and in any case their own balance-of-payments position will not deteriorate as long as their domestic inflation is not materially above the average rate of their principal trading partners.

A key-currency country suffers no such constraint, certainly not in the short run; its main constraint is the risk that it may ultimately lose its key-currency status. In the meantime the annual additions to world holdings of its currency are not entirely net additions to reserves-to-hold (true or digested reserves, held because the holder wants them as a hedge against future contingencies); instead they are to a large extent additions to reserves-to-spend (undigested reserves, holdings in excess of perceived needs). The demand for true reserves is largely a function of money income in the receiving country; rising money income is virtually the only factor tending to convert the available supply of reserves into desired reserves; and under today's conditions "rising money income" is virtually synonymous with inflation.

Not to mince words, the problem now relates specifically to the U.S. dollar. All these things have happened to that currency, starting in the late 1950's, by which time Japan and most of Europe had largely restored the competitiveness of their economies. Foreign exporters still accept dollars because they can sell them to their central banks even if they are in surplus in foreign-exchange markets. * The monetary authorities of other countries will accept them because they are conventionally counted as part of external reserves and may be used to meet a balance-of-payments deficit of their own in the future if the need arises (which is what external reserves are for). Some countries, however, eventually found their external reserves were entirely adequate already, yet were

---

* When a country is running a balance-of-payments deficit you normally expect its currency to be weak in foreign-exchange markets, as was the case with the U.S. dollar through most of the 1970's, but the weakness can be offset by other factors. The dollar has been persistently rising in terms of other currencies since October 1978 in spite of continuing deficits, because U.S. interest rates have been high and many U.S. borrowers are considered good credit risks, so there has been a strong net inflow of financial capital that has buoyed up the exchange rate.

unable to use their continuing earnings of dollars without upsetting the foreign-exchange markets, so they had little choice but to hold excess dollar balances indefinitely. In effect, they have had to make forced loans to the U.S.A.

The Multiplication of Reserves

However, the monetization of the U.S.A.'s balance-of-payments deficits (financing them by issuing more dollar balances to nonresident holders, i.e. by creating additional international reserves) is not the end of the story: it may generate a further multiple expansion of such reserves. The dollar balances created in this way provide additional cash reserves to offshore banks, and will lead to still more dollar balances with those banks (Euro-dollars or offshore dollars) by a sequence of loans and redeposits that is exactly parallel to the process by which domestic banks expand their deposits when their cash reserves increase, as briefly described in the third section of this chapter. Other countries may borrow offshore dollars to meet their own balance-of-payments deficits, or they or their residents may do so for normal capital purposes, or U.S. business firms may borrow there instead of from domestic banks, and a substantial portion of these funds will tend to be redeposited with offshore banks.

Furthermore, this expansion of offshore balances will be beyond the control of the Federal Reserve System as long as U.S. balance-of-payments deficits continue. The total supply may therefore be determined, within rather imprecise limits, by the international community's appetite for borrowed reserves. *

It is only under certain unfavourable circumstances that offshore balances escape the control of the central bank of the home country (in this case the Federal Reserve System). Unfortunately, these unfavourable conditions are very much part of the financial scene today. First and foremost is the weakness of U.S. exports: if they were fully competitive

---

* For a parallel in the domestic economy, imagine a situation in which the commercial banks can expand their cash reserves at will. This was actually the case in many countries from the end of World War II into the 1950's, when commercial banks held large portfolios of government securities accumulated in the course of wartime financing, and central banks were pegging the prices and yields on them: the commercial banks could expand their reserves at will by selling off securities that the central bank was obligated to buy at set prices. In the U.S.A. this situation persisted until the 1951 "Accord" between the Treasury and the Federal Reserve Board ended the pegging of government securities prices and restored the Board's control over commercial-bank reserves. In other countries essentially the same solution was found, usually with rather less publicity, at about the same time.

in world markets then borrowed reserves and earned reserves alike could be readily converted into goods and services, and excess balances in the hands of nonresidents either would not exist or would be quickly eliminated. Second, the great expansion of offshore banking in recent years has correspondingly expanded the credit-creating capacity of the world financial system, weakened the control of national monetary authorities over their own currencies, and increased the availability of U.S. dollars for international-reserve purposes. (Or, since chronic U.S. balance-of-payments deficits have greatly favoured the growth of offshore banking, you might say they have contributed indirectly as well as directly to the international spread of inflation.) Third, international borrowing for balance-of-payments reasons has become common and eminently respectable—and quite rightly so, of course, within reasonable limits, since it gives the borrower time in which to effect necessary economic adjustments. (Unfortunately, however, it also permits some borrowers to postpone necessary adjustments indefinitely; and of course it leaves all borrowers vulnerable to a serious downturn in the world economy.) Finally, in the 1970's the major international commercial banks concluded that loans to sovereign nations were not only highly profitable but also relatively riskless, given the readiness of the international community to acquiesce in the practice.

To recapitulate, we have already seen that there has been a double relaxation of the controls that used to operate automatically on the money supply: an external-reserve medium in elastic supply (an inconvertible key currency) has been substituted for one in relatively inelastic supply (gold, or a currency convertible into gold); and the direct link between the external reserves and the domestic money supply has been abolished. Now add a redundant supply of the key currency, and Parkinson's Law of Reserves virtually guarantees world-wide inflation.

The World Debt Crisis

Two paragraphs back we noted that the major international banks got into so-called "sovereignty" loans in the 1970's, when they appeared to be relatively riskless. The points at issue there were two: (1) the ease with which these loans could be raised was largely due to the liquidity that the U.S.A.'s balance-of-payments deficits injected into offshore financial markets, because of the key-currency role of the U.S. dollar; and (2) the additional lending-and-spending thus made possible generated additional inflationary pressures in the world economy. By 1981, however, a third problem had appeared: international bankers were getting increasingly nervous about the safety of some of these loans. In 1982 it became public knowledge that many countries were facing major difficulties in meeting their obligations, and that the problem was so serious as to constitute an immediate threat to the solvency of many banks and to the functioning of the international financial system as a whole. Intensive negotiations between lenders and borrowers began, which brought a series of debt moratoria, reschedulings, and other adjustments that is still not over as this is being written. Disaster has been avoided, and will probably continue to be avoided, for both lenders and borrowers stand to lose heavily if defaults become widespread, but the basic problems have not yet been solved.

What went wrong? What are the basic problems? Were the world's leading bankers, usually thought of as highly cautious and conservative, guilty of making irresponsible loans?

Well, since bankers are as human as the rest of us, it would be surprising if they had not made any mistakes at all. Nevertheless there can be no doubt that the main cause of the trouble in most cases was the set of restrictive economic policies followed by most industrialized countries since about 1975 in an effort to control inflation, which were intensified in the 1980's. These policies are the subject of Chapter 9. Before dealing with that issue, however, we need to explore the domestic aspects of inflation in greater depth.

Chapter 5

THE MICROECONOMICS OF INFLATION

Price Determination

Price determination is in the field of microeconomics, i.e. the field of relative prices of particular goods and services, the field of supply and demand, which was once the main concern of economic analysis. It deals with questions such as why diamonds are valued more highly than bread, what determines wage rates in general and wages in various lines of work, why rent is paid for the use of land, how the earnings attributable to a particular piece of productive machinery can be calculated, and that sort of thing. Ever since the 1930's it has been largely overshadowed by the great and glamourous advances in the field of macroeconomics, but it may be due for a major revival as we try to fathom the reasons for the impasse that macroeconomics has led us into, after the major advances it seemed to be delivering in the early years after World War II.

You may be surprised to find that, for all we economists talk of prices and the price mechanism in a money-and-market economy, we really know very little about how prices are actually set in the real world. The model of pure competition offers only a highly generalized abstraction of the process. It sees the price of each commodity or service as being set by the interaction of supply and demand, usually represented by schedules or graphs or mathematical functions. At any given state of technology, suppliers are willing to offer greater total output at successively higher prices; their costs may at first decline as output increases, because of economies of scale, but will then begin to increase for a variety of reasons. With any given set of tastes and preferences, buyers will be prepared to pay a high price if the available supply is small, and will then restrict their use of that commodity or service to its most important applications; as availability increases they will be prepared to use it more freely, but only at progressively lower prices. At some level of output the price buyers are willing to pay will just cover the sellers' costs; that point will determine both the price and the level of output.

Unrealistic as this model is in many respects, it does capture important relationships among costs, output, prices, and consumption. Certain modifications of the analysis throw up supplementary points of some moment. A concept sometimes known as "externalities" is an example, though concrete instances usually involve significant departures from the conditions of pure competition. The basic point is that the actions of one firm or individual may impose costs on others which they may not be able to reclaim from that firm, or may confer benefits on others for which it can not exact a price—i.e. some costs and benefits may be **external** to the firm and therefore it does not take them into account in deciding whether the benefits from its action will justify the costs. For example, the smelters that emit sulphur dioxide and nitric oxide into the air themselves suffer only a negligible part of the damage done to the economy by the resultant acid rain, and so do not consider it when computing the profitability of their operations; and a proposed dam might not only provide a means of generating electricity but also control seasonal flooding downstream from the site, yet a public utility might conclude that the project was uneconomic without considering the downstream benefits because they would not contribute to its revenue. Clearly, some modification of the free-market solution in such cases would be in the public interest.

The pricing process envisaged in the model of imperfect or monopolistic competition improves considerably on that in the older model. The typical firm is insulated to some extent from price competition, and its prices are "administered"—the firm sets them unilaterally at whatever level promises to be most profitable on a going-concern basis. Thus it may refrain from raising prices during a boom, to maintain customer goodwill, but on the other hand it may not reduce prices in a slump for fear of spoiling its markets for the future. Also, it will presumably be spending money on advertizing and sales promotion of various kinds, and will factor those costs into its prices. Naturally its prices will have to take account of those set by its nearer competitors, but there is often room for material differences. This is a considerable advance in realism, but still far short of a full explanation of real-world pricing, about which we will have more to say in the next chapter.

Motivation, Profits, and Efficiency

In the model of pure competition the main motivating force is that each participant tries to maximize his net return. For workers this means neatly balancing hours of work with hours of leisure, so the real incomes they could earn by working a little longer just offset the enjoyment of a little more leisure. For the owners of property it means seeking the highest yields they can get on their property or investments. For entrepreneurs it means seeking a maximum pure profit. However, these returns need not be measured exclusively in money or goods. For example, some people prefer to be in business for themselves even though their net incomes are less than they could earn as employees of someone else; evidently they prefer the psychic income they get from being their own bosses to the additional real income they could otherwise earn.

The motivating forces in the model of imperfect or monopolistic competition are less clearly identifiable in the case of the entrepreneur. Indeed some economists doubt that this function is present at all in the relatively large firms that are typical of this model; the matter then becomes one of what motivates the firm as a separately-identifiable entity. (Others argue that individuals identifiable as entrepreneurs still have their place, but exercise their function by gaining control of the firm and bending it to their will.) Some minimum level of profitability is certainly a necessary feature of the firm if it is to survive at all, and some minimum rate of return to the owners (or hope of an eventual return) is necessary over time. However, the owners and the managers of a large firm are not necessarily the same people (as they presumably are in the model of pure competition), and their interests may differ in important respects. Nevertheless the maximization of net returns is by no means the only possible game plan, whether we think of the net return to the owners, the net return to the managers, or the net return to the firm regardless of how it is divided between owners and managers. Other possible goals may be some desired rate of growth of assets or output; maintaining or expanding the firm's current share of given markets; penetrating new markets; or outperforming a particular rival.

The common perception of a monopoly is that it is able to exact excessive* profits (presumably meaning profits in the broad sense, not necessarily pure profits). This perception may carry over to firms in the model of imperfect or monopolistic competition, but it is not necessarily accurate in either case. In the model of pure competition, all producers must sooner or later adopt the most cost-efficient methods currently known or go out of business, but that does not apply in the newer model. Being sheltered in part at least from price competition, and perhaps motivated by other goals than maximizing their net returns, profits may be eroded in at least three possible ways. First, they may be appropriated by a strong management, especially if ownership is widely dispersed among the general public. Second, they may be appropriated by some or all employees in the form of higher wages and fringe benefits, if they are in a strong bargaining position; or they may be more-or-less voluntarily dispersed by management in the same way, in order to promote good industrial relations. Third, potential profits may be dissipated through

---

* Usually measured by comparison with the profits that would have been generated if the output had been produced and sold under the conditions of pure competition.

the tolerance of lax or inefficient productive techniques. With sufficient insulation from the activities of competitors, established routines and techniques may not be questioned even though they may have been outmoded by newly-developed alternative routines and techniques.

A Pragmatic Approach

Traditional microeconomic views of price determination offer little insight into the economics of inflation, for they are primarily concerned with **relative** prices and rely on a supplementary construction (the quantity theory) to explain the general price-level. All the pricing procedures dealt with in the preceding sections of this chapter could readily be expressed in terms of some standard commodity such as wheat rather than money (as classical economists were wont to emphasize). The one point that does have an identifiable link to inflation is the last one, namely that potential profits may be dissipated through inefficiency. In this case, however, the causal sequence seems to run the other way: inflationary conditions make it easier to pass on increased costs in the form of higher selling prices, and hence may give further encouragement to inefficient production practices. Thus there would appear to be little hope of devising a permanent anti-inflation program that will be fully compatible with our money-and-market economy until we know a lot more than we do now about how prices are actually set in the real world.

We can not afford to wait until the economics profession comes up with a satisfactory model of the pricing process and integrates it into the general body of economic theory—The Fearsome Dilemma is far too pressing for that. In the meantime a pragmatic description may help, even though it can not claim wide professional acceptance, but is purely personal and subjective instead. It begins with the "bid" and "asked" prices to be found in organized markets for securities and commodities where trading occurs in standard board lots. When such markets attract many buyers and many sellers, the procedure does closely resemble an auction market: the spreads between bid and asked prices are likely to be narrow, and "the" price at any given moment can be clearly identified with considerable accuracy. For most transactions by the general public, however, a better analogy is a thin market in which there are relatively few sellers, or few buyers, or both. The spread between bid and asked prices may be wide, and trading may be infrequent with rather wide swings in prices (if buyers and sellers are few and have about equal market power), or may be persistently at either the bid or the asking side (if one buyer or one seller dominates the market).

Typically, a would-be seller will set an asking price that he believes will give him the maximum net return, limited primarily by the fact that too high a price will leave him with an unwanted inventory of unsold goods or services. Note that this applies to the sale of all sorts of things by all sorts of people—a manufacturer selling physical goods, a public utility selling a service of some kind, a professional man selling legal or medical or other services, a wholesaler or retailer buying and reselling either goods or services, a wage- or salary-earner selling his services to an employer, a labour union bargaining on behalf of its members, and so on. Also, it applies regardless of whether the seller is a monopolist controlling the entire supply of what he is selling, or must compete with others (whether few or many) offering the same or similar products.

For his part, a would-be buyer must be prepared to set a bid price for anything he wants. In some cases this may be a firm price he is unwilling to exceed, especially if he is the only buyer (a monopsonist) or the most important buyer in that particular market. Even if he has little market influence, however, he must make up his mind about what he is prepared to pay—perhaps after finding out what typical sellers are asking. Naturally, any bid he is prepared to make will be biased towards the lowest price he can hope for.

Obviously, no trading can take place until some buyer decides to pay some seller's asking price, or until some seller decides to accept some buyer's bid price. Major business firms may have considerable monopolistic power over their selling prices, and perhaps some monopsonistic power in buying goods and services. Spectacular confrontations sometimes occur when a monopolist negotiates with a monopsonist, or when each side has considerable market power, as when a strong labour union negotiates a wage contract with a major employer. For most of us, however, it means selling our labour to the employer who offers us the best terms we can find, and buying our needs from whatever nearby retailers post the lowest asking prices; as a rule the choices open to us at any given moment are limited, though we may be able to wheel and deal a bit when buying or selling a used car or a house or some other thing in transactions with other individuals.

As an individual, your welfare is strongly bound up with your money income. You can add to the total real income of the community as a whole by working harder, turning out more goods per hour or getting more done, but your own real income may not increase one iota—the immediate benefit may go to your employer or to someone else. If you can get more money for the same amount of work, however, then your real income will rise almost exactly in proportion; any conceivable increase in your personal money income can add only infinitesimally to inflation. If you are an employee, therefore, you will be sure to propose the highest **asking price** you can hope for when hitting the boss for a raise. Pretty much the same applies if you are a manufacturer selling some product you have made, or a professional man selling specialized services, or a seller of just about anything.

Realized prices are something else again. If market conditions are favourable you easily get your asking price—and then wonder whether you should have asked for more. If market conditions are unfavourable, however, you may have to choose between accepting much less than your asking price and not making the sale at all. Of course, much will depend upon how strong your bargaining position is, and whether you have resources to fall back on. If you have enough savings set aside, or if you are eligible for unemployment insurance benefits, you may choose to reject a job offer at a relatively low wage in hopes of getting something better later, even if that means a period of unemployment. If you are a businessman and sales are slow, you may be able to absorb losses for a while without cutting your selling prices, hoping not to spoil your market for the future. If you want to sell your house but don't have to move right away, you may be content to wait till you get your asking price. All of which helps to explain why prices tend to be very sticky in the face of downward pressures, but tend to rise easily when the opportunity offers.

Now suppose many people raise their asking prices for what they want to sell "tomorrow" by a hefty amount, more or less simultaneously. Except as they are willing to draw down past savings, all they will have to spend will be the money they earned "today", which will not be enough to buy the same output at the newly-increased prices. Something will have to give. Some temporarily unemployed people who expected to find another job as good as or better than their last will find it difficult to get a new one of any kind. Inventories of unsold goods will accumulate. There will be cutbacks in production, idle or underutilized plants, and layoffs. Money income will fall, and the spending stream will become even less capable of buying the old level of output. For the economy as a whole, therefore, excessive asking prices spell reduced output (i.e. reduced real income) and unemployment.

The adverse economic climate will of course put downward pressure on all asking prices, but it may be a long time before realized prices will ease materially. In fact asking prices may continue to creep up, because costs will still be rising as previous price increases at earlier stages in production work their way through the economy, and because reduced volume will mean that overhead costs must be spread over a smaller output. If monetary policy is tightened, as it well may be in order to combat inflation, increased interest rates will add further to business costs. Realized prices may also continue to rise, for those who still have jobs will find that their money incomes are rising more or less in step with prices. If fiscal and monetary policies are eased, the main immediate effect will presumably be to reduce unemployment, but it will soon add to inflationary pressures too, because it will validate more asking prices and will encourage sellers to maintain strong pricing strategies.

The Public Interest

Now look back at the discussion of "externalities" in the first section of this chapter. To put it a bit differently, the interests of the general public are not necessarily well served by leaving all decisionmaking to the supposedly-impersonal forces of the marketplace. In the days when most economists thought the conclusions derived from the model of pure competition could be applied fairly directly to the real world it seemed good enough to rely on the discipline of competition to regulate most prices; in the relatively few cases where the private costs did not reflect the full social costs, or where social benefits exceeded private gains, it appeared that the balance could be restored fairly easily by taxes or subsidies or other forms of government intervention—taxes on a polluter, subsidies for a utility to reimburse it for downstream benefits not otherwise captured in its revenues, and the like.

However, don't run away with the idea that externalities affect only business enterprises like smelters and utilities: they affect you, me, and virtually everyone else in the community, regardless of how we earn our living. If you are a wage- or salary-earner and you are offered an increase in your pay that more than covers the increase in prices since your last raise, will you refuse it on the grounds that it will be inflationary? You would certainly be unusually conscientious if you did so, though when negotiating with your employer you (or your union on your behalf) might very well refrain from making demands you thought clearly unjustified. Nor is it at all clear in most cases that you should decline the increase, no matter how conscientious you are. You can reasonably expect to share in the increasing productivity of the economy as a whole, and an increase in your money income is the principle way of doing so; your skills or knowledge or general usefulness may have increased; you must consider the needs of your dependents; and if the increase is freely offered or is the result of bargaining in good faith then it seems to be justified by the normal rules of the marketplace.

Well, what about a professional man who perceives that his clients will now pay him substantially higher fees than before? Isn't that evidence that the marketplace is putting a higher value on his work?

What about a landlord who sees an opportunity to raise his tenants' rents? A businessman who sees an opportunity to raise his selling prices by much more than his costs have risen? An investor who finds his interest and dividend receipts rising? Well, a humane landlord may be reluctant to raise his rents, but as he senses that his tenants' incomes are rising with inflation and as his own costs rise too the time will come when he will act. Some businessmen may indeed refrain from raising their selling prices as much as they could. But all these people will be able to claim, with some justification, that in raising their fees or selling prices or in receiving higher investment income they are just accepting the verdict of the marketplace; they will not likely see any direct connection between their good fortune and the inflation that plagues the community as a whole, or if they do they will not likely feel that anything they did or did not do would affect it much one way or the other. Nevertheless the combined effect of all these individually-insignificant actions is to impart a strong inflationary bias into the economy.

The Fearsome Dilemma raises an entirely new conflict between the private and the public interest, between the limited effects considered by each individual decisionmaker and the total effect on the economy, between "internalities" (as we may call them) and externalities. Each price-setter remains free to set whatever price he thinks is in his own best interests, knowing full well that others are doing likewise but oblivious to the inflationary implications. However, his attitude is only partly due to the realization that restraint on his part will have a miniscule effect on inflation unless everyone else does likewise. It is also influenced, consciously or unconsciously, by past experience, which indicates that the authorities will act to accommodate a good part (though perhaps not all) of these collective pricing decisions, because too draconian a restraint on the spending stream would add materially to unemployment. The net effect, of course, is a combination of inflation no-one wants with painful unemployment. Until recently it seemed that the worst any seller had to face was a period of slow sales, not a new depression like the 1930's; by now, however, depressed conditions have lasted for a decade, and unemployment has reached levels not seen for over 40 years.

Chapter 6
REAL-WORLD PRICING

The Marketing Approach

Some real-world prices are set or monitored by independent regulatory bodies, usually government agencies; skillful representations before these bodies will be important to the producer, and will involve costs of preparation and presentation. Other prices are set by noisy public confrontations, as when wage rates are negotiated between a strong labour union and a major employer; gamesmanship is evidently involved on both sides. But the majority of pricing decisions are made discreetly in the conference-rooms of individual business firms. What is the basis on which they are made?

Marketing textbooks identify prices as simply one component, though an important component, in a philosophy that approaches economic activities from a holistic rather than from a production orientation. The product itself, the channels by which it will be distributed, its pricing, and promotional activities are the four major elements in a firm's marketing strategy; the last-named may well be the most important in many cases. One author defines marketing as "a total system of interacting business activities designed to plan, price, promote, and distribute want-satisfying products and services to present and potential customers".[1] Management is expected to find the best combination of these elements for reaching its goals. The design of the product must obviously be appropriate for the intended market. However, it may have to meet specific price limitations if it is to sell at all. If it is to be sold through middlemen it may have to be supported by one or more related products; for example, appliance dealers may insist on a full range of complementary items. Promotional considerations may also affect the design of the product, its packaging, the selection of a brand name, and related matters.

In this philosophical framework the question of pricing is more likely to be approached as a matter of "How much can we get for it?" than "How much must we ask in order to cover our costs?" Pricing decisions are certainly important, especially for items that must compete with a number of close substitutes, and the seller must be prepared to alter his prices quickly if he finds he has misjudged the market or if conditions change. It is easier to reduce a price if necessary than to raise it, so the initial decision is likely to be on the high side—especially if the product has new features that may be expected to attract quick interest.

Generally speaking the final price to the ultimate customer must cover all legitimate costs, otherwise the product (and perhaps the firm as well) will not survive, though there are exceptions: some products may be used as "leaders" to bring in other business, or may have to be offered to fill out a standard range of related products despite low sales volume, in which case their selling prices may not cover all the costs that may be attributed to them. However, "cost" turns out to be a rather slippery concept. For pricing purposes it must be reduced to a per-unit-of-sale basis, but it is often difficult to determine per-unit costs accurately even for a past period, let alone to predict them for the future periods for which pricing decisions must be made. Prudence therefore dictates that selling prices be based on rather pessimistic cost projections, if competitive conditions permit.

Business costs may be divided into manufacturing costs, transportation costs, and selling costs. The old adage has it that if you build a better mousetrap the world will beat a path to your door, but in practice very few products indeed are sold exclusively through word-of-mouth advertizing by satisfied customers: money and effort must be put into marketing them. And someone must pay for transporting the product from the producer's plant to the premises of the buyer; some portion of this cost may be paid by the purchaser himself, even if it is no more than the time and effort you spend in doing the grocery shopping and carrying your purchases home; other portions may be paid by middlemen, such as wholesalers or retailers; but in some cases the producer may pay some or all of it.

Manufacturing Costs

Manufacturing costs include all legitimate expenses necessary to put the finished product in the warehouse of the producer, ready to be shipped to customers. (The customer in this case need not be the final consumer, of course; he may be another manufacturer, for whom the first firm's product is simply raw material for further processing, or he may be a wholesaler or a retailer.) These costs are made up of a number of rather different components. One important category is overhead costs, meaning general or "indirect" costs that can not be allocated to any one particular operation, like the rent (or the amortization of the cost) of a building that is used for more than one purpose, insurance, and "indirect" labour (remuneration of management, clerical staff, etc.). Other categories may be specific to a particular operation, including "fixed costs" (the capital cost of the necessary plant and machinery) and "variable costs" (such as "direct" labour and raw materials). As their name implies, variable costs vary closely with the volume of current output, but once a building is built or a machine bought it becomes a "sunk cost" that can only be recovered as it is charged against subsequent production or written off out of income.

Other complications arise because the typical firm produces more than one product. Some of these may be joint products, like the many distillates derived from a barrel of crude oil, and their joint costs may have to be allocated rather arbitrarily among them. In any case all overhead costs must be allocated among the firm's products, and fixed costs must be apportioned over the useful life of the capital items which give rise to them. The usual life of a machine may sometimes be estimated in terms of the number of units of output it will produce before it wears out, in which case the amortization of its cost works out at a constant or virtually-constant rate per unit, but alternatively it may be necessary to amortize it at a set rate per annum regardless of whether it is run constantly or not at all. In either case there is also the possibility that new and better machinery will be introduced that will make the old machine obsolete before it is worn out, so that risk must be factored into the cost estimates as well.

Furthermore, estimating the probable volume of sales (and therefore of production) may be critical to making the right choice of productive technique. Often there is a choice of two, three, or more known procedures that may be used, and which is the most cost-efficient depends on the expected volume of output. A simple example is the issue of a written memorandum. If it is to go to only a few people, then carbon copies or photocopies may be the most economical way of handling it. For a larger circulation, mimeographing or offset printing. For a very large circulation, typeset copy and a high-speed printing press.

Even variable costs may prove less predictable on a per-unit basis than their nature suggests. Delays in the receipt of raw material, accidents, breakdowns, labour unrest, and other factors not (or not entirely) under management's control may conspire to slow down the rate of output and raise per-unit costs. Material prices and wage rates may rise more rapidly than expected, especially in an inflationary environment.

This recital of costing problems is not intended to create a great mystery, for standard accounting practices solve many of them quite satisfactorily, and a going concern will soon accumulate enough experience to give adequate day-to-day guidance on the others. Rather, the point is merely to emphasize that the per-unit manufacturing cost for a given product is difficult to estimate accurately in advance, without any consideration of other costs. In fact it would be fair to say that a per-unit cost is a target rather than a known datum. This is particularly true of products for which fixed and overhead costs make up a large part of total per-unit costs, as in the automobile industry: per-unit costs depend heavily on production volume; production volume (which must approximate sales volume) depends on selling price and on promotional expenditures; hence decisions on output, selling price, and marketing expenditures must be carefully coördinated. This is exactly what led to the original concept of "administered" prices: the term was first applied to a situation in which coördinated decisions of this kind were required. The solution was to make the best possible estimate of how many units could be sold at each of a number of different prices and what would be the most cost-efficient production technique at each of those production levels, pick the most promising combination, then mount a sales campaign to sell at least that many units at the indicated price. If the projected break-even point were not reached then the losses might be substantial, but if it were exceeded then overall profits would rise sharply indeed.

Manufacturing costs exemplify the concept of cost that the model of pure competition is built around, for this is where the introduction of new and more cost-efficient productive techniques can materially increase output and reduce costs. New techniques may involve dramatic new inventions, but they may also involve much more mundane changes: the improvement of existing equipment, better maintenance procedure, better materials-handling methods, standardization of work patterns, and so on. The accepted term to cover all these possibilities is **innovation**. Some innovations may be capital-intensive, such as the use of highly automated equipment, others may be very simple but more cost-efficient ways of organizing the productive process.

Some "manufacturing" functions in the sense we have used the term may be performed by firms we do not normally think of as manufacturers. For example, in some cases wholesalers may buy products in bulk, repack them in smaller quantities, and sell them to retailers. Importers commonly perform such functions on goods bought abroad, including relabelling them to suit domestic market requirements. Retailers, too, may participate, especially in providing some of the transportation services that get goods delivered to the ultimate consumer, and in servicing appliances and other equipment on behalf of the original manufacturer.

Transportation costs are subject to pretty much the same considerations as manufacturing costs—you may think of them as the cost of manufacturing the service of transportation. They may be paid for by the prime manufacturer and recovered in his selling prices, or they may be the responsibility of the purchaser. Another possibility is that they may be performed by a wholesaler or retailer as part of the process of distribution. In some cases they may be performed as an entirely separate business activity, as when a pipeline company buys oil outright from producers, transports it to market, and sells it for its own account.

Essentially similar "manufacturing" costs are incurred in producing the intangible services that are an important part of total output in a modern economy—medical, dental, and other health services, legal services, financial services (insurance, banking, security-trading, etc.), barbering, hairdressing, other personal services, and the rest. Even if we disregard the money the professional man has invested in specialized education, on which he expects a reasonable return, these services require substantial capital investment in equipment of various kinds, and continuing expenditures for the hire of competent staff, the rental and furnishing of suitable premises, the purchase of supplies, etc. Essentially the same costing problems arise for them in setting their fee schedules.

Selling Costs

With few if any exceptions, a firm at any point in the production and distribution of goods or services will incur selling costs in marketing its products. These costs may include advertizing in any of a variety of ways, the sponsorship of sporting or cultural or charitable events, the wages, commissions, and expenses of sales-promotion staff, and various forms of allowances and discounts offered to firms further along the chain of distribution (e.g. wholesalers or retailers) for handling the firm's products. As with manufacturing costs, selling costs are most familiar to us as they apply to physical goods, but they also apply in the service industries.

It is a common practice to make all or part of a salesman's compensation in the form of a commission calculated as a percentage of sales, perhaps combined with more-or-less generous allowances for travel and other expenses. Indeed, most or all employees whose work is reasonably closely related to sales-promotion may be included: sales supervisors may get overriding commissions on the sales of those whose work they supervise, district sales managers on all sales in their district, right up to the Vice-President in Charge of Sales. Some firms confine the selling and distribution of their wares to their own staff, who deal with final consumers on a door-to-door basis; they are likely to have highly structured sales organizations. Others may sell through normal whole-sale and retail channels, in which case their own directly-employed sales organization may be less elaborate. In some cases the firm may endeavour to control prices right through to the consumer level, including the markups wholesalers and retailers make ("resale price maintenance"), though such practices are severely limited in some jurisdictions: where they are permitted, the seller (usually but not necessarily the prime manufacturer) may offer more generous markups than his competitors in order to encourage dealers to push his products. Even where wholesalers and retailers buy the goods outright and resell them for their own account, or if resale price maintenance is prohibited, it is a common practice for them to determine their selling prices by adding a standard markup to their buying prices. The wholesaler or retailer may also be given an "advertizing allowance", and perhaps some specific sales material, to encourage him to include the manufacturers products in his own local advertising.

The various commissions, markups, and allowances that go into a typical selling price to the final consumer are pretty firmly set by agreement or custom, so they constitute a major element of rigidity in the price structure. Exact figures are hard to come by, for they are sensitive trade secrets jealously guarded from competitors, but in total they often amount to a substantial portion of the final price. Retail markups are known to be particularly high in furniture and other high-priced and relatively-slow-moving businesses, which is not surprising since the cost of holding and displaying inventory is high. Promotional expenditures add further to total selling costs. In book-publishing the rule of thumb is that the selling price must be five times the cost of printing and binding; the difference is made up partly by the author's royalty (typically no more than about 10 percent) but mostly by commissions and markups at various levels, advertising, and other selling expenses. Another line in which selling costs appear to be particularly high is pharmaceuticals, for markups are generous and promotional expenditures are high.

Of course, as already noted, some of the commissions and markups allowed to middlemen may cover expenses that ought to be considered as manufacturing costs rather than selling costs. Nevertheless purely-promotional costs are high in many lines of business—some firms have reported expenditures approaching 50 percent of sales revenues, not including advertising or personal selling.[2] New firms or new products require high initial outlays for promotion, related to expected future sales rather than current sales. However, the periodic introduction of new or improved products is a common marketing technique, aimed at the continuing creation of new wants; in such cases promotional expenses are likely to account for a large portion of selling prices at all times. Also, an established firm may make it a practice to plow back a given percentage of sales revenues into advertising and other promotional channels in order to maintain or expand its share of the market.

Sales Techniques

The model of pure competition assumes that productive efficiency is the only significant way of achieving success in business, and that putting a lower price on a product of given quality (or offering products of better quality for the same price) is the only form of competition in the marketplace. In the real world, however, things are generally quite different. There are many other forms of competition besides price competition, and they are often of greater importance. In fact consumers are often surprisingly unconcerned about price differences, or even contemptuous of them. To some extent this is quite rational; who would drive (let alone walk) a mile to save 50 cents on a $2.50 item he buys only rarely, even if the saving is an impressive 20 percent? In other cases it may be a matter of prestige, or a demonstration of unconcern for material things.

Nevertheless, competition with respect to price and quality is indeed important in the real world, and no seller can allow his prices to get very far out of line with his close competitors without risking a material loss of sales. This is especially true of things we buy regularly, like staple food items: differences between prices at competing food stores are likely to be small. However, quality comparisons are involved, and judgments about quality are notoriously arbitrary. Furthermore the average consumer just cannot afford the time and trouble and expense of carrying out extensive comparisons on an objective and scientific basis. For occasional purchases of a large and costly article, like an automobile, he may do serious comparative shopping. For the most part, however, he will find that the balance of advantage lies with finding a reasonably-satisfactory brand of toothpaste or razor blades or whatever and sticking to it. Consumer testing organizations offer some help in evaluating big-ticket items that are infrequently purchased, and many others that are bought regularly, but the number of consumer products is so great that it is impossible for them to cover all items and keep their reports fully up to date.

In many lines of business competition in providing "service" to the customer largely replaces competitive pricing, and "price cutting" may be looked on as unethical behavior on the part of the merchant. Cheerful and helpful sales personnel are indeed a very real factor in customer satisfaction. So are effective and well-distributed facilities for repairing or maintaining all sorts of consumer durables, from automobiles to boats to mobile homes to large and small household appliances, not forgetting such essentials as furnaces, oil burners, and plumbing installations. In some parts of the world it is more important when buying (say) an automobile to select a dealer that maintains an efficient repair-shop and a good parts inventory than to select a make or model that is highly rated by consumers' organizations. Nevertheless "service" in any of these senses is usually secondary, and should not be allowed to seduce us into paying higher prices or accepting poorer quality in the product we are buying.

Another sales technique has already been noted: a manufacturer may offer retailers or wholesalers a higher-than-normal markup on his products, in order to encourage them to promote his wares over those of rivals. Overt practices of this kind are probably rather rare, because the likely result is simply to persuade competitors to raise their markups too, but the importance of wholesaler and retailer goodwill is probably sufficient to ensure generous markups in those lines where they are controlled by the manufacturer. Secret rebates to favoured merchants offer a more subtle form of the same technique, and may be hard to detect. And of course the pressure for a special "deal" may come from the other side: large chain retailers may be able to drive hard bargains with certain manufacturers, perhaps on the grounds that their large-scale purchasing offers economies of scale to the seller. In this case the discount may be quite legitimate, and the benefit **may** be passed on to the final consumer in lower prices, but on the other hand it may be merely a hidden way of giving the retailer a higher markup for pushing a certain line of goods.

In many lines of business it is common to provide nationwide or even worldwide chains of retail outlets for the product or service. Examples include supermarkets and other chain retail stores, gasoline service stations, banks, hotels, restaurants, fastfood outlets, pharmacies or drug stores, dry-cleaning and laundry establishments, and many others. Multiple outlets may indeed offer some economies of scale through joint administration, quantity purchases, and the standardization of efficient procedures. From the point of view of the individual consumer, of course, there is also some advantage, because multiple outlets make it more likely that he will find one conveniently located for his needs. But they also trade heavily on one of the major factors behind brand loyalties that we have already noted: the advantage of sticking to a known product instead of experimenting with a new one that may or may not prove better, since comparative shopping does involve real costs to the consumer.

Multiple outlets have additional advantages for the seller, however, which do not benefit the consumer. In practice they help him maintain (and, he hopes, expand) his share of the market by providing surplus capacity in a variety of locations in anticipation of future market growth. Even if his hopes are not fulfilled in every case, the law of averages works in his favour. Also, adding a new outlet before its capacity can be fully utilized may forestall a competitor from pre-empting a favourable location. From the point of view of the community as a whole, however, there are serious disadvantages—unfavourable externalities, to use the term introduced in the first section of Chapter 5—in that continuous operation at less than capacity represents wasteful use of resources.

Even where wholesale and retail operations are in the hands of independent merchants, there may be factors at work leading each to operate at less than full capacity. Freedom of entry at the retail level, for example, is likely to lead to a multiplicity of outlets competing for a limited volume of business. Many new ventures are started each year on the basis of high hopes and low capital, and a high percentage of them fail before long. The practice of allowing standard markups and the common tradition amongst merchants against price-cutting may protect each firm from cut-throat price wars, but new competitors are soon attracted by signs of success, which are hard to disguise, and volume at each outlet is thus held down to a level that no longer attracts new entrants. No-one gets "excessive" profits in any sense, but there is unnecessary duplication of investment in premises and inventories.

Advertizing in one or more of its various forms is a virtually-universal sales technique. At its simplest it may be no more than a means of informing potential customers about what goods or services the adver-tizer offers, which is certainly a useful service. Who has not had the experience of learning in this way about some useful product or service he did not even know existed, perhaps from merely walking through a store and observing a display of goods for sale? Or learning that some product or service he wanted was available from a source much nearer by than he knew of? Information of this kind must be counted as a net addition to real income, because it yields benefits the consumer did not know were available at all or because it saves him time and trouble in supplying himself with them.

At the other extreme, advertizing may be merely persuasive: it may persuade us that we "need" things that are inherently useless, or that Brand A is materially superior in quality or usefulness or durability to all competing brands even though in fact it may be no better whatever, perhaps inferior, and higher in price to boot. Human beings are highly suggestible, not to say gullible, and prone to do what "everyone else" is doing. Why? Well, we'll have to leave it to the psychologists to explain it. Perhaps it is some residual remnant of the herd instinct, or the reflex actions that cause the individual members of a flock of birds or a school of fish to participate freely in joint manoeuvres and sudden changes in direction that do not seem to have any rational motivation detectable by an independent observer. Such responses, after all, do seem to have been an important part of the mechanism by which the accumulated wisdom of the ages has been transmitted from one generation to the next for humans as well as other animals, though humans have gradually come to learn by thought and analysis as well, thanks to the maturing of their intellectual powers. Whatever may be the explanation, however, the facts are hardly in dispute: smooth-talking individuals through the ages have been able to persuade their brethren to part with their birthright for a mess of potage. We laugh patronizingly at stories of the wiles of snake-oil salesmen and other carnival touts in an earlier age than ours, yet we blithely buy a particular brand of breakfast cereal because some slick presentation on television tells us to, or respond mechanically to subliminal advertizing messages, or follow arbitrary dictates about what we should wear because "it is the style".

In practice, of course, a typical firm will make simultaneous use of a number of these sales techniques, perhaps all of them. They are complementary rather than alternative ways of promoting sales.

A Ratchet Effect on Costs and Prices

In the real world there is indeed some scope for reducing manufacturing costs and selling prices as a means of expanding the market for a given product, as in the imaginary world of economists' models: small computers and other electronic gadgetry offer many dramatic examples in recent years. Even in today's inflationary environment the prices of highly-manufactured goods have usually risen relatively slowly, while the prices of food, raw materials, and relatively simple manufactures have risen more rapidly. But the immediate opportunities for greater sales and greater profits are far more likely to lie in increased expenditure on sales-promotion than on cost-cutting, even in highly-manufactured goods. Typically, a substantial portion of costs in any line of business consists of fixed costs and overheads, including current commitments to advertizing and sales promotion as well as the overheads described above for manufacturing costs, so any increase in sales will reduce average costs per unit of sales; a successful sales campaign may thus produce a substantial immediate increase in profit at relatively moderate cost.

An increase in spending on sales-promotion designed to expand sales or market-share may be described as an **offensive** tactic. Competitive firms are likely to respond in kind, i.e. to employ **defensive** sales tactics.

The net effect on total sales of competing products is likely to be a zero-sum game: if one supermarket gains it is likely to be all or nearly all at the expense of lost sales for other supermarkets. Even if there is some net gain in supermarket sales, it is likely to be at the expense of reduced sales in some other type of retail establishment. Thus a substantial portion of all sales-promotion budgets is merely offsetting or merely defensive: any firm that falls behind its competitors in expenditures of this kind may expect to lose some of its market share, perhaps a substantial part of it, and any firm that increases its expenditures can only hope to gain if its competitors fail to respond aggressively. At best the market is likely to be in unstable equilibrium, because each firm will be tempted to increase its sales-promotion expenditures by as much as it feels it can "get away with" short of stimulating a general escalation, so there will be a tendency for the selling costs (and therefore the total costs) of all participants to creep upward. Thus we have another example of unfavourable externalities: what is to the advantage of the individual firm results in the waste of resources for the community as a whole.

If the general price level is being held stable in some way, then any price increase brought about by the struggle for increased market shares must be offset by reductions in prices elsewhere—perhaps losses for or bankruptcies of some firms in the same industry, perhaps in other industries. However, the mere fact that prices remain stable does not mean that the public interest is unaffected. On the contrary, from the point of view of the general public it is clear that a substantial (and perhaps increasing) portion of the community's total resources is absorbed in an unproductive struggle by individual producers to maintain their market shares.

As noted in Chapter 5, it does not necessarily follow that "profits" will be excessive in any sense, or that any employee or supplier will get more material rewards than in any other comparable employment. Rather, imperfect competition typically leads to higher-cost operations from which no-one gets any real benefit. There is a Parkinson's Law of Costs too: costs tend to rise to absorb the available revenue. The costs of maintaining an adequate inventory can be very heavy, especially at the wholesale and the retail levels and at today's interest rates, but any one merchant will suffer lost sales if he fails to stock an adequate volume of a wide variety of items. This one factor alone insidiously raises the real cost of operating too many wholesale or retail outlets at less than full capacity: the waste of resources can be enormous.

An instructive example of how this sort of cost-escalation can mushroom is to be found in the current passion for erecting new shopping centres or shopping plazas or shopping malls throughout North

America—a passion that appears to be spreading even farther afield. Now, in itself the idea of a shopping centre is an excellent one: it is a real service to consumers to have a wide variety of shops in close proximity, with adequate parking space for automobiles and good public transportation. Originally the idea was to have only complementary shops in any one centre—one supermarket, one department store, and a number of specialty shops—but experience showed that this was too restrictive; it turned out that two or more similar shops in the same centre may generate enough additional trade to benefit all participants. The new centres did, of course, draw some business away from older downtown business areas, but that was merely a case of obsolescence due to innovation. Soon, however, the shopping centres themselves began to proliferate. The big retail chains were induced to open branches in new centres, even though they competed with established branches in other centres still not operating at capacity, because each chain feared to let its rivals get into too many of the new centres. Now we have underutilized shopping centres full of underutilized retail outlets.

Who benefits from the plethora of shopping centres? Well, the public gets some increase in conveniently-located centres, it is true, but at heavy cost in increased overheads that must be covered by higher prices. The real beneficiaries, of course, are the promoters. A promoter scouts out a likely new location, assembles the land, draws up a plan, and begins to line up participants. If he is skillful and persuasive he may even raise mortgage financing for **more than 100 percent of the cost**, for the land he has assembled is now "obviously" worth much more than he paid for it, considering the pending development of the site. He includes some glamourous new features designed to make the public feel privileged to shop in a grand new shopping centre but pay no more than at competitive outlets elsewhere. Then, that project completed successfully, he moves on to scout a new location, oblivious of the fact that it will draw a significant portion of its clientele from other shopping centres that are still not used to capacity. Another example of unfavourable externalities.

Towards a Cure

It is thus easy to construct a plausible hypothesis about inflationary biases in real-life pricing policies. However, broad generalities of this kind do not really get us very far towards a solution; we need specific information, or any action we may take may do more harm than good. Selling costs may need careful monitoring, but they can not be slashed arbitrarily, because within proper limits they are very functional. Advertizing benefits consumers by informing them of products and services they might not otherwise know about and by enabling them to get more satisfaction (i.e. more real income) from a given money income. Markups for wholesalers, distributors, and retailers cover important economic functions such as maintaining adequate inventories, providing transportation and distribution services, and others. A multiplicity of conveniently-located retail outlets is certainly an advantage to the consumer. In all cases the problem is to identify the costs and the benefits accurately, and to insure that the interests of the general consuming public are properly served. We want to reduce or eliminate the merely-competitive components of selling costs, the wasteful duplication of facilities, and that sort of thing, without hampering the efficient operation of private enterprise.

To that end we need further factual information about manufacturing and selling costs and about pricing policies, at least in major industries. What are the critical factors in successful market strategies? How are the decisions made on interlocking questions about productive techniques, output targets, selling costs, and selling prices? How are distributional markups determined? What services are rendered and what costs are incurred by various participants in the chain of production and distribution? Only when we have answers to these questions will we be in a position to make sound judgments about the validity of any given practice and about how to improve on it.

Chapter 7

THE MACROECONOMICS OF INFLATION

Demand Management

The way economists today look at major economic totals like employment, real output, real income, money income, and the general price level for a nation or a region—the macroeconomics of that nation or region—has evolved out of a more-or-less-continuous process of theoretical debate and practical applications of the principles so derived, which began in the 1930's and is still far from complete. The principles thus worked out may be said to have cured The Great Depression of those years through what has come to be known as demand management. The "cure" was not instantly concocted in one piece nor introduced effectively as of any one point in time by the application of precisely calculated doses of a scientifically compounded remedy. Rather, its composition and application were stretched over many years of trial-and-error experimentation. World War II was inadvertently a major part of the process, because of its immense drafts on the economic resources of belligerents and neutrals alike, but for the same reason it introduced major distortions that complicated the transition to peacetime conditions throughout the world. A fairly broad consensus was achieved by the year 1950, though that consensus was never complete and was visibly disintegrating by (say) 1970.

Let us begin with the initial successes of modern demand-management policies in overcoming the depression, or in assuring a relatively smooth transition from wartime to peacetime conditions after the end of hostilities in 1945, whichever way you prefer to express it. The principles involved can be simply illustrated if we think of the productive process as a circular flow of physical goods and services (real income or real output) from producers to consumers, coupled with a flow of money payments in the opposite direction (the spending stream) which regulates the flow of real output. At each stage in the process someone buys raw materials or partly-finished goods from someone else, pays for the labour and other services necessary to advance production a stage further, and sells the product to someone who is prepared to continue the process, until finally it is bought by the consumer in the form of food, clothing, durables, or other goods or as educational, health, or other services. The consumers who buy these goods and services are the producers who participate in the productive process, and the income with which they purchase them is the sum of the receipts as wages, salaries, and investment incomes that accrue to them because of that participation.

If the spending stream holds steady then the current output of goods and services can be paid for at current prices out of current money income, but if it falters for any reason then output declines, money income declines in consequence, and a deflationary spiral may set in. That is basically what happened in the 1930's. The weak point in the circular flow is that people do not spend all their income on consumption, they save some of it. That is not a bad thing in itself, but a potentially good thing: the rising standard of living in the world over the past 200 years at least can be attributed in large part to investing these savings in new productive capital goods that have permitted more and more output to be produced with a given workforce. However, the public's willingness to save merely **permits** new capital investment, it does not **ensure** it. To avoid deflation, aborted income, and aborted saving, the money some people want to save out of a given income must be borrowed and spent by someone else; and there is no obvious reason why would-be investors would want to borrow just the amount savers want to save.

Economists used to think that the interest rate could be relied on to keep the current rate of saving and the current rate of capital spending in balance. They (or most of them) thought that people would save less and spend more if the rate of interest fell, and that capital spending would increase, because there seem to be all sorts of useful capital goods that could be built if only the interest costs were low enough. Either one of these responses, and certainly the two together, should be enough to ensure that the spending stream would hold steady. But in the 1930's **neither** of these things happened. Interest rates did not fall at first, or not very much, because people with money to lend were afraid to do so for fear of losing their capital. Many people saved more rather than less, even though interest rates eventually did fall, because they were afraid for the future. And lower interest rates did not persuade businesses to add to their existing plant and equipment, because the facilities they already had were not being fully used. Pretty much the same pattern is being repeated in the 1980's.

After much turmoil and heartsearching among economists, politicians, and the general public, a new approach to the problem (summarized in section 6 of the Appendix) gradually became widely accepted. Even yet there is not full agreement on all the details, and the early optimism has faded somewhat as the dimensions of The Fearsome Dilemma have become plainer, but the broad essentials seemed clear enough in the 1950's. It became recognized (as some economists had argued long before the 1930's) that the rate of saving is not very clearly related to the rate of interest; it is now usually accepted as a given datum for most purposes, more clearly related to income than to anything else, but influenced by many other considerations and subject to change over time, sometimes quite sharply. Capital spending plans are certainly influenced by interest rates, but by many other factors too, especially the expected profitability of the particular project. Modern demand management does make use of the interest-rate effects of monetary policy for whatever stimulus they can give to capital spending in slack times, and to discourage it when it appears to be excessive, but it does not rely exclusively on these effects. Monetary policy also directly influences the spending stream, because it affects the **supply** of lendable funds as well as their **price** (the interest rate). Ideally, this will channel all savings into housing and productive capital, mostly in the private sector, but fiscal policy can compensate for any difference. If private borrowing-and-spending is insufficient then government borrowing-and-spending may be increased by tax reductions or new spending. If total spending threatens to be excessive then the government may budget for a surplus.

Looking back at the 1930's with the benefit of hindsight, we may conclude that the troubles experienced in those days were greatly worsened by policies that were the exact reverse of demand-management techniques. On the best economic advice then available, the authorities in country after country acted to reduce instead of to expand the spending stream. The economic theorists of the day could offer no explanation for general and chronic unemployment, but they had plenty of experience with economic disturbances in a given country that got overextended for some reason or other—usually inflationary excesses. The remedies that had cured many cases of the latter type of malady—belt tightening, balancing the government's budget, and deflation—were all they could prescribe for the former. And prescribe they did, in the apparent belief that "overextension" had somehow occurred. If similar circumstances occurred nowadays, we would initially count on the automatic stabilizing effects of falling tax receipts and rising government spending on certain services to cushion the deflationary spiral, and would soon reinforce those effects by tax cuts and new spending projects; then, governments tried to reduce spending and increase taxes. Now, we would encourage public and private employers to operate as normally as possible in order to support the spending stream; then, wages and salaries were cut repeatedly in both the public and the private sectors.

Considering the magnitude of the economic adjustments facing the world at the outset, demand management must be acknowledged to have operated with remarkable success in the first 20 or 25 years after the end of World War II. The needed adjustments included not only the repair of direct war damages in countries that had been the scene of military actions in the recent conflict and the correction of related distortions in other countries, but also the legacies of events stretching from World War I to The Great Depression; for over 30 years conditions had never been "normal" in any meaningful sense. There were real and widespread fears that the world would soon lapse once more into depression, still a painful recent memory in most people's minds, but instead there began an expansion of the world's real income and of international trade that eclipses anything known to past history.

Inflation was of course recognized as an ever-present risk under the immediate circumstances, and it did occur from time to time on a serious scale in some countries as the authorities struggled to increase the output of consumer goods and services and to dismantle the direct controls that had kept inflation repressed during wartime. Nevertheless it was widely assumed, at least as a first approximation, that inflation would not be a continuing problem unless expansionary policies were pushed too strongly once full employment was reached or closely approached; "price stability" was mainly interpreted as the avoidance of renewed deflation. And for a long time practical experience seemed to justify this belief. In many countries prices rose by no more than one or two percent per annum (dubbed "creeping inflation"), and it seemed reasonable to expect that others could do as well in due course. Only a few Cassandras were warning against the disruptive effects of inflation at this low rate, and feared that it would get worse.

Demand-Management's Achilles Heel

What went wrong? After that auspicious start, why are we now plagued by The Fearsome Dilemma?

There is an all-too-human tendency to look for someone else to blame when things go wrong, and in this case there is no doubt that serious criticisms can be levied against some of the economic policies followed by the two major Western powers, Britain and the U.S.A. Britain is entitled to some discounting of these criticisms, because of the severe physical and financial beating it took in the war and because it is still torn by what can only be described as economic class warfare, yet there is no denying that some of its postwar policies were shortsighted and selfish: we need look no farther than its reluctant and belated participation in the European Common Market. The decision of the U.S. government to fight the Korean War with little or no increase in taxes—to try to have butter as well as guns—was a major factor in the upsurge of world inflation in the early 1950's, thanks to the key-currency status of the dollar. After 1957, by which time the application of free-enterprise principles and liberal trade practices at U.S. urgings had brought European and Japanese reconstruction to the point where their products were again competitive on world markets, the U.S.A. turned protectionist instead of following its own competitive prescription for prosperity. And the U.S. role in the collapse of the international monetary system in the 1970's was not constructive. Interest-rate policies in most countries were also open to criticism, as will be argued at the end of this chapter.

Whatever criticisms may be made of U.S. policies in this era, however, it is important to remember the powerful and unselfish leadership and help given to the world by successive U.S. administrations in the first dozen years after World War II. These enlightened policies contributed a great deal to the regeneration of the productive capacity of the world as a whole, including its greatest industrial rivals, friend and foe alike, on a scale that is without historical parallel. They were a concrete expression of faith in the free-enterprise system and in the virtue of healthy competition.

In any case these criticisms can not explain why the promise of the early years of demand management has not been fulfilled. There must have been some fundamental weakness in demand management itself to have brought us to our present pass, for any practicable economic strategy must be able to adapt to an appreciable range of human errors of judgment in its execution. Evidently its architects greatly underestimated its vulnerability to inflation. They had no immediate concern with that problem, for it was deflationary pressures and unemployment that commanded their attention. Inflationary pressures did build up in most countries during and immediately after World War II, but in principle they ought to have ended when sufficient progress had been made in the transition to peacetime conditions. Demand management was designed to keep the national economy from slipping back into chronic depression, but it was also supposed to be equally effective in forestalling the emergence of excess demand, which everyone realized would lead to inflation. Now, however, we have inflation **without** excess demand.

Demand management pursues several explicitly-stated economic objectives simultaneously, prominent among which are price stability, a high level of employment, and a viable balance-of-payments position, as noted towards the end of Chapter 1. The first two—the domestic policy objectives—are the critical ones, for it is pretty clear that the third would be relatively easy to attain for all countries if they could achieve a reasonable approximation to the first two. Freed from the horns of The Fearsome Dilemma, every country could expand its real output until its full productive potential was realized; the main deterrent would be an adverse shift in its balance of payments, because some portion of its increased money income would be spent on imports. But this "import leakage" from one country would provide a net economic stimulus to other countries, so their incomes would rise and there should be a favourable feed-back effect on the first country; if all were to follow expansive policies more or less simultaneously, then none should suffer seriously-adverse balance-of-payments effects.

Of course it would be sheer coincidence if this put every country's external receipts and payments neatly in balance; there would probably be a persistent drain of reserves from some (deficit) countries to other (surplus) countries, which could be tolerated temporarily but not indefinitely. However, under the postulated circumstances it should be possible for the international community to agree on relatively simple measures, such as a realignment of exchange rates, that would shift some resources from export sales to domestic sales in the surplus countries and from domestic sales to export (or import-competing) sales in the deficit countries, because effective high-employment policies would facilitate the transfer of resources from one industry to another without causing more than temporary adjustment problems.

It follows that the solution to The Fearsome Dilemma must be sought by each country within its own borders. However, a solution that will work in one country should work in others also. In principle there is no reason to doubt that any country, large or small, might pioneer in this breakthrough, but as a practical matter the main responsibility rests on the major industrial powers precisely because of their greater economic capabilities.

Economists now generally acknowledge that there are two necessary conditions for the successful pursuit of several independent policy goals: (1) there must be at least as many independent policy instruments as independent policy goals, and (2) progress towards each goal must be capable of being influenced by at least one policy instrument.[1] (This is a little like having to have as many independent equations as unknowns in solving an algebraic problem, but in this case we may need more "equations" than "unknowns" because some of the "equations" may be weaker or less reliable or subject to greater margins of error than others and so may have to be reinforced.) However, a little thought should persuade you that there is a third necessary condition, though this one is less-widely recognized in economic literature: (3) it must be possible to influence progress towards each goal independently of progress towards all other goals, otherwise our efforts to achieve one goal might either cause us to overshoot another or negate our efforts to attain it.

Demand management can boast a considerable variety of policy instruments—monetary policy, tax policies, government spending policies, debt-management policies, and so on, some designed to help particular groups such as farmers or fishermen or homeowners or to promote particular activities such as oil exploration, others designed to influence economic activity in general. That seems to meet the first requirement for effective economic management. Both monetary policy and fiscal policy (or the two main components of the latter, tax policies and spending policies) directly influence the spending stream and therefore influence progress towards both major domestic goals, so the second requirement is clearly met. However, though each can do things the other can not, monetary and fiscal policies overlap to a considerable extent because they both operate primarily by expanding or contracting the spending stream. Furthermore the spending stream is not in itself a policy goal but merely a means of achieving the two major domestic goals; and it can not influence progress towards one without also influencing progress towards the other. The spending stream directly affects real output and thereby affects employment, but it also affects prices, because it determines the flow of money income, out of which all money payments in the economy must come.

Clearly, the third requirement for effective demand management is not met. Powerful as they are in controlling the spending stream, monetary and fiscal policies can not control its subdivision into a quantity component (real output and the level of employment) and a price component. If employment and prices are both weak, as was the case in the 1930's, then increasing the spending stream will promote both goals. If prices are rising despite unemployment, however, as they are now, then increasing the spending stream **may** bring greater output and employment, but it may merely validate a higher price level—in all probability it will do some of both. Nor can any other presently-known policy instrument or combination of policy instruments isolate the price and the quantity effects either.

You may at once contradict that last sentence and assert that **effective** price and wage controls would indeed permit the price and the quantity components of the spending stream to be treated separately, and ensure that any increase in it would go entirely into expanding output and employment. True enough, in the short run at least, **if** the controls could be made really effective and **if** they did not create new problems of their own. We will return to this subject in Chapter 10, where we will express serious doubts on both counts.

A New Kind of Inflation

A good case can indeed be made for believing that the inflations that now plague the world are categorically different from those known before, but not because of cost-push pressures, which are nothing new. One obvious difference is that inflation is now virtually a world-wide phenomenon, and the inflation in any one country evidently has clear links to the inflations in other countries. A more subtle and more important difference is that, with a few notable exceptions, national inflations can no longer be ascribed to weak or inept governments unwilling or unable to levy adequate taxes, nor to inadequate controls over private borrowing from the banking system, nor to a surge of urgently-needed expenditures that drives even strong and competent governments to resort to inflationary financing. Rather, even countries with strong monetary and fiscal systems and the most sophisticated modern demand-management techniques seem unable to restrain their domestic inflations under stable peacetime conditions.

Deficits in government budgets are widely in evidence, it is true, but they are not deficits of desperation. Monetary expansion is certainly a factor in today's inflations, but not because that is the only feasible way of financing the budgetary deficit nor because of inadequate controls over the financial system. No, the authorities could indeed pursue more restrictive fiscal and monetary policies than they are now following, were they not deterred by The Fearsome Dilemma. In most peacetime inflations of the past, inadequate monetary or fiscal policies (or both) were the spearhead of the attack on price stability; now the monetary and fiscal authorities are fighting a heavy rearguard action against upward price pressures that seem to have a life of their own. Britain and the U.S.A. have led the way in government-expenditure-cutting on a scale not seen since the ill-starred retrenchments of the 1930's, combined with restrictive monetary policies that have raised interest rates to record levels not only in nominal terms but also in real terms, i.e. after deducting the current rate of inflation, and a number of other countries have followed fairly closely behind. So far inflation has slowed down somewhat, but only after a long delay, and unemployment and idle productive capacity have risen above anything seen for over 40 years.

In the bad old days the money supply was fixed in relation to gold reserves or to some other arbitrary standard, and governments were expected to balance their budgets at all times. The economy's money income was pretty much a zero-sum game: if one person or group got more, some other person or group got less, because the spending stream was effectively limited by the quantity of money and its velocity of circulation. However, the limit was neither very precise nor very satisfactory. In boom times it might become surprisingly elastic, thanks to modern credit facilities, and an appreciable inflation might get under way. Sooner or later, however, something would set off a scramble for cash that would not merely end the expansion of the spending stream but actually reduce it. The finite limit on the money supply did not really control inflation effectively, it merely ensured that the periodic bouts of inflation would be more or less offset by periodic recessions or depressions.

Demand management evolved out of our efforts to free ourselves from the boom-and-bust cycle, and it changed the rules in two important ways. First, it cut the link between the money supply and that "barbarous relic", gold; we can now set it at whatever level we feel "the needs of trade" require. This replaces a fixed limit on the money supply by a flexible limit, but in itself makes relatively little difference; the authorities can still limit the money supply as effectively as ever when they deem it necessary. The second change in the rules is much more important: our policy objectives and priorities have changed. Central banks were expected to make a concerted effort to smooth out the business cycle under the old rules, but preventing inflation had priority if any conflict of objectives was perceived. Nowadays, however, the authorities are expected **both** to combat inflation **and** to maintain a high level of output and employment. Neither objective has absolute priority. Demand management came so close for so long to achieving both at once that we can no longer accept the full rigour of traditional anti-inflationary policies as a necessary catharsis. If a conflict between the two is observed—as it certainly has been in recent years—the authorities must exercise their best judgment. That means a significant portion of the price increases sellers are asking will be validated by an increase in the money supply and in money income. The authorities are fully aware that allowing the money supply to increase will release additional inflationary pressures, but not doing so will mean that some part of the potential output must go unrealized (or that the unrealized potential already in evidence will increase) and unemployment will be worsened. **That** is what makes today's inflations categorically different from those of the past.

Why Did Success Turn to Failure?

"Hold on there!", you may say, "If that is really how the system operates, how is it that demand management worked as well as you say it did at first? Why have things got so much worse since then?"

There are four factors that help to explain what has happened:

- Persistent fears of a relapse into chronic depression undoubtedly had a sobering effect on everyone's asking prices in the early postwar years. Memories of the 1930's gradually faded, however, and were replaced by growing confidence in the new system.
- Our growing wealth and the improved cushion of social-security benefits has steadily raised most people's ability to hold out for something closer to their asking prices. Business capital has increased, and credit is easier to obtain, so a typical firm has greater resources to see it through difficult periods.
- Once people realize that prices are likely to rise persistently, they alter their asking prices accordingly. When all prices are rising you are not taking much of a risk if you do let your asking prices get a little ahead of your competitors: you may suffer slow sales for a while, but other prices will soon catch up and put you back onside.
- When this process gets started, it tends to accelerate. In the 1950's most people preferred to believe that creeping creeping inflation was harmless if not actually beneficial. Then it gradually became clear that the authorities could not crack down too severely on prices, because that would aggravate the unemployment situation. Price demands got bolder. Soon it was seen that nice guys were coming in last. Being a nice guy has now gone out of fashion in this league.

Other Opinions

The macroeconomic analysis summarized in the preceding sections of this chapter, and the account of demand management in particular, is based largely on the Keynesian economic model described in section 6 of the Appendix. In Chapter 3 we referred to the controversy between monetarists and Keynesians, and mentioned some of the points of disagreement; section 7 of the Appendix gives a little more information about monetarist views. However, monetarists and their kinfolk are not the only ones to criticize the way demand management has operated in practice; even many economists who fully accept the general principles of the Keynesian analysis have disagreed strongly with some of the policies that have been followed. For the most part these controversies and differences of opinion involve matters that are far too specialized to be treated within the limits of this book, but three of them are of sufficient general interest to merit formal acknowledgement here.

Some disciples of Keynes began quite early to promote a low-interest-rates-no-matter-what philosophy with what can only be described as religious fervour.* Their views gained rather wide acceptance, which was surely an important factor in letting inflationary forces generate the impressive momentum that eventually forced major policy changes in the 1970's. As recently as the start of that decade most major nations were stoutly resisting the upward pressures on market interest rates, even though creeping inflation was accelerating and had already made many real interest rates negative. (Germany was a notable exception, and was roundly criticized for it by her trading partners—also for not inflating at the same "gentlemanly" rate as they were.) Some economists even then argued that more realistic rates would make for a healthier economy, but they were ignored. (Was it mere coincidence that Germany, with higher interest rates and lower inflation, was especially prosperous and successful?) By now the doctrinaire belief in low market interest rates has been thoroughly discredited. Monetarist critics certainly played a major role in the matter, but many nonmonetarists (including professing Keynesians) also contributed.

Some perspective on the interest-rate controversy may be gained by noting that there is a long tradition in economic theorizing that identifies a "natural" rate of interest. It is a "real" rate, unaffected by inflation and independent of the market rate; it is governed by income, saving, capital formation, and other factors measured in physical rather than merely nominal or money terms. Nominal changes, such as an increase in the money supply or in bank lending, may cause the market rate to depart from the natural rate, but equilibrating forces will be set in motion that will tend to bring the two together again. The analysis was originally based on the model of pure competition, but it survives the transition to more sophisticated models reasonably well. Thus monetary policy in the Keynesian model may be taken as operating primarily on nominal or market interest rates, without denying that forces might thereby be set in motion tending to restore the real rate. Indeed, if an easy-money policy and low interest rates help to revive a depressed economy and stimulate

---

* There is nothing in the Keynesian analysis as such to say interest rates should always be kept low. Without meaning to suggest that Keynes is the final arbiter on all aspects of the model he pioneered, it should be noted that his *General Theory* was addressed to conditions of deep depression. **Under such conditions** it is indeed logical to keep interest rates as low as possible, not because that is likely to do much good in itself, but to encourage any revival of private capital spending that may occur if profit expectations revive. Under other conditions, however, high interest rates may be entirely appropriate—for example, to restrain an inflationary capital boom that is overextending the economy. The major thing to be avoided, it would seem, would be erratic ups and downs of interest rates over a substantial range within a relatively short period, for that would undermine the market for the long-term issues needed to finance long-term projects.

new private capital formation, or if tight money and high interest rates help to cool off an overheated economy, it would be logical to expect nominal rates to move back towards the natural rate. You might say that demand-management policies involve a deliberate manipulation of market interest rates, but real rates do fight back.

A more serious difference of opinion centres on unemployment. Monetarists deny that involuntary unemployment can exist (except perhaps temporarily—and their most recent writings seem to deny it can occur even temporarily). They postulate a natural rate of unemployment, like the natural rate of interest, and deny that monetary policy (or anything else) can prevent the observed rate of unemployment from returning to the natural rate. If they are talking about a long-run-equilibrium position, their argument makes a lot of sense: their natural rate of unemployment seems very much like the rate other economists see as the minimum feasible level, because of normal job turnover, frictions, seasonal factors, and the like. However, as noted in Chapter 3, monetarist analysis seems to identify real-world conditions with long-run-equilibrium conditions. But the long-run-equilibrium position is itself a highly abstract conception—it may be interpreted as arising at the end of an indefinitely-long period in which all existing disturbances or disequilibria work themselves out and no new disturbances are allowed to occur. Conclusions drawn from a model with the explicit and implicit assumptions on which this analysis is based are highly suspect for real-world applications.

One pair of authors has asked, "Are there any economists who feel that most of today's unemployment is voluntary and that, if offered a job at the going or a slightly lower real wage, most of [those] out of work would say 'no'?".[2] Yet that is what monetarists are claiming.

A more subtle criticism of Keynesian macroeconomics has been advanced by the late Maurice Lamontagne, an able Canadian economist and political figure: that it ignores the extensive analytical material on business cycles painstakingly assembled since the early years of the 19th century.[3] At the end of World War II business cycles was recognized as a major field of study within the discipline of economics; now it gets minor attention, because it has been overshadowed by the Keynesian model. Three major cycles are generally recognized, plus a number of lesser ones, all operating independently. First there is a short cycle of about three years, often associated with the name of Joseph Kitchin; it is an inventory cycle, caused by overreactions of suppliers to minor fluctuations in consumer spending. Next is an intermediate cycle of about ten years duration, which the general public identifies as "the" business cycle; it is associated with the name of Clement Juglar, and its principal cause is variations in capital spending. The third is a long cycle of forty or fifty years, associated with the name of Nikolai Kondratieff; its causes are less well established, and some economists suggest it may be a series of unrelated historical accidents rather than a consistent set of events, but it is clearly identifiable in many statistical series.

The Keynesian revolution in economic theory pretty well brushed all this aside: demand management has focused on keeping the spending stream stable with little regard to the nature of possible disturbances. Nevertheless the forces that tend to generate cycles of various kinds are deeply rooted in the money-and-market economy, and the appropriate countermeasures for them are quite different. Moreover, social and psychological factors clearly play an important role not only in cyclical processes but also in all aspects of economic activity. Economic policies could undoubtedly be made more effective if greater attention were paid to these matters.

Chapter 8
THE REDISTRIBUTION OF INCOME

Factor Costs, Factor Returns, and Income

In Chapter 3 we identified human labour and productive property as "factors of production." Traditional economic theory separates the latter category into two, land (or natural resources in general) and capital goods, but the distinction is not very meaningful for our purposes since in either case the owner of the property in question receives a share of the income it has helped to create. From the point of view of the enterprise that employs these factors in a productive process, the payments for their use are factor costs. Any given firm's selling prices can be resolved into (a) payments for the purchase of materials and services from other firms, (b) wages and other personal emoluments, and (c) payments to the owners of productive property. However, the first category can be resolved into the same categories for the sellers, so all business costs can ultimately be identified with the second and third categories. This exercise is routinely done in computing the figures for net national income at factor cost in the national accounts. *

From the point of view of the recipient, these payments are factor returns: in the one case wages, salaries, commissions, professional fees, and all other forms of personal remuneration, including the wages of management; in the other rents, dividends, retained profits, and all forms of investment income, including capital gains. In this guise they constitute the total income out of which the economy's total output is purchased. Thus factor returns determine how income is divided in the first instance—not merely the division between "labour" and "capital", but also the shares that go to individual wage- and salary-earners and to the owners of particular pieces of property. Incomes from sources not

---

*The more commonly-used series, gross national product at market prices or GNP, includes (1) depreciation or capital-cost allowances, i.e. allowances for the replacement of capital used up in the productive process, and (2) indirect taxes, which are not "real" costs to the community because they are not paid for any necessary productive inputs, but merely use the market mechanism to divert real income to cover part of governmental expenditures. Deducting depreciation from GNP gives net national income at market prices; deducting both depreciation and indirect taxes (such as sales taxes, paid by producers but passed on to the consumer as higher prices) gives net national income at factor cost, which is an attempt to measure income in universally-applicable terms. (For example, it is unaffected by whether governmental revenues are raised by direct taxes or indirect taxes.)

directly related to productive activities do not constitute a net addition to the income of the community, they merely shift some of it from those who actively participate in production to the ultimate beneficiaries; the shifts are usually effected through government taxation and expenditure accounts, and are known as transfer payments. *

Economic theory can tell us how a community's income will be divided up if specified conditions exist, such as the private ownership of all or most productive capital; how it **ought** to be divided up is another matter, for it involves value judgments on which equally rational people may profoundly differ. Socialists say all or most productive property ought to be owned by the state on behalf of the general public, or by regional or local governments in the case of facilities serving purely regional or local needs, or in some similar way, so everyone will benefit equally. Advocates of free enterprise argue that private ownership under reasonably-competitive conditions makes for greater efficiency, so there is more income to divide up and everyone is better off; in other words, they say inequality of income pays dividends in the form of greater productivity. The mixed economy now obtaining in much of the world bypasses the question of ownership and substitutes *ad hoc* measures of income redistribution, thus trying to get the best of both worlds.

Economic policymaking in any country, democratic or other, must be based on enforceable general principles about how its income is to be distributed among its people. A totalitarian regime may enforce a distribution based on anything from unfettered free enterprise to complete socialism, provided only that the results are acquiesced in by the populace. A democracy must find some sort of consensus, perhaps a compromise among many differing shades of opinion. Political stability requires that those who disagree with the current distributional formula must be prepared to work through constitutional channels to effect the changes they wish to bring about; serious dissatisfaction with the *status quo*, or with the speed with which improvements are being made, may lead to violence or revolution.

The Erosion of Past Achievements

In the past 200 years what we are wont to call Western Society has enjoyed a phenomenal growth in real income and in the welfare of the populace as a whole. A major factor has unquestionably been the evolution of the free-enterprise system based on money, markets, and

---

* Technically, interest payments on money borrowed for consumption or other nonproductive purposes are transfer payments. In the hands of the receivers, however, it is not usually feasible to separate out those interest payments that are transfers rather than factor returns, and for our purposes the distinction is irrelevant.

freedom of contract, which replaced feudalism and mercantilism. These developments have contradicted the predictions of early critics of the new system—of whom Karl Marx is the best-known but by no means the only example—that its shortcomings would prove so serious that it could not long endure. Their expectations ranged from chronic stagnation through "inevitable" replacement by a process of dialectic materialism to bloody revolution, with varying emphasis on such factors as gluts of unsalable goods, recurring and worsening crises, massive unemployment, and increasing misery for the masses.

These critics had no way of foreseeing the major redistribution of income through social legislation that has persistently accompanied the process of industrialization under the free-enterprise system in democratic countries. It can be cogently argued that this largely explains why their dire predictions were negated, and therefore that it has made a fundamental contribution to both economic growth and political stability in what is now the mixed system of free-enterprise-with-government-intervention that characterizes Western Europe, North America, and much of the rest of the world. It can be further argued that the repressions and revolutions so painfully evident in Latin America and elsewhere offer further support for this thesis: the ruling elites may skillfully use the rhetoric of democracy, but they have no intentions of letting the reality of it be practiced in their countries, nor of permitting any significant redistribution of income, so the adverse consequences foreseen by 19th-century critics are indeed evident.

Prior to the evolution of demand management, social intervention to ameliorate the workings of the money-and-market system merely redistributed whatever real income happened to be produced in good times or bad. This was accomplished in part by progressive taxes and in part by government transfer payments out of general revenues for approved purposes or to support the incomes of certain groups or individuals. The progressivity of the tax system depends heavily on income taxes,* though 19th-century reformers had placed much faith in death duties, which they hoped would gradually reduce the disparities of income as well as those of wealth and thereby promote equality of opportunity. Transfer payments include expenditure on education, health services, social insurance plans of various kinds, children's allowances or family allowances, assistance for the physically or mentally handicapped, support for the income of primary producers such as farmers and fishermen, provision for the indigent, and many other programs. At first they were

---

* Other sources of government revenue—sales taxes, property taxes, fees, etc.—have disproportionately-high incidence on lower incomes and are therefore regressive. Studies in some countries indicate that the overall tax system is at best proportionate, despite progressive income taxes.

offered mainly by private charities, but the involvement of the state began to expand in the late 19th century. Their scope has persistently increased over the years, and in many countries the pace of change accelerated markedly after World War II. With the rise of demand management, however, an entirely new dimension was added: official intervention came to address not merely the redistribution of a given level of income, but also the effective use of all available productive resources for the realization of all potential real income. Effective policies of this kind add greatly to the welfare of the working population and materially reduce the incidence of poverty.

Advances in social legislation have always met with resistance, and they are never irreversible. To some extent this is desirable: like other things in this imperfect world, many programs and proposals prove to be deficient in one way or another, and some are bound to be mistaken or to need revision. No matter how sound a particular measure may be, however, the probability is that it will impinge unfavourably on some vested interest or other, and hence will face persistent efforts to modify or abolish it. Thus death duties have lapsed into insignificance in many jurisdictions, and are rather easily avoided in others, and many ingenious tax shelters for investment income have been introduced—usually justified as devices to stimulate investment in desirable projects or in preferred forms, but clearly eroding the progressivity of the tax system. Tax planning has become a growth industry; consultants openly advertize their skills at finding havens or loopholes that will minimize the bite of the tax collector on investment income. And of course it is the wealthy client who stands to gain from their efforts: the average citizen with limited resources can benefit little, and the poor can not benefit at all. The marginal tax rates on high incomes at the end of World War II would clearly have been counterproductive if continued in peacetime, and in most countries were promptly reduced in the early postwar years. However, the process has been continued ever since, though somewhat irregularly.

Dating from the 1978 summit meeting of the major powers or thereabouts, the erosion of redistributional measures has accelerated. Demand management has been emasculated in the effort to control inflation. The curtailment of government expenditures is everywhere the order of the day. In many jurisdictions reactionary governments have come to power, and have stepped up the process of modifying or rescinding existing social legislation. Where tax reductions have been made, they have favoured high incomes rather than low; the unemployed get little but kind words. Even liberally-minded governments have fallen in line with the current fashion.

Income Distribution in Troubled Times

It is difficult enough at the best of times to maintain or improve an existing consensus on income distribution, but inflation really puts the cat among the pigeons. As noted in Chapter 1, it distorts the pricing mechanism on which most decisions depend in a money-and-market economy. The pattern of income distribution is affected in ways that are not always obvious. In principle inflation favours debtors (or at least those debtors whose obligations were contracted before the implications of inflation were fully recognized) and penalizes creditors, but some in both categories fare better than others. Market interest rates rise as inflation becomes recognized and its implications affect new debt contracts, but the net effects on any particular borrower or lender vary greatly according to his tax status—some borrowers find that the tax collector shoulders part of their burdens, whereas some lenders must pay tax on their nominal interest income even though its real value may be low or even negative. Shrewd speculators often reap huge profits, while patient merit fares badly. Wage- and salary-earners can usually protect themselves fairly well by demanding (and getting) increases approximating the rate of inflation, but disparities between earnings in various activities may increase: those in the strongest bargaining position do best. Government budgets may be under pressure despite rising revenues, because the costs of existing programs will be rising too, so it may be difficult to undertake new programs no matter how worthy.

Deflation, of course, has painful effects that are more or less the reverse of those imposed by inflation, but in addition it brings substantial unemployment. Debtors find that obligations assumed in good faith in easier times suddenly become far more onerous, for it will take more output or more hours of work to repay them. Interest rates may not decline, or may even increase because of the greater risk of default, and even if they decline the debtor may not be able to renegotiate his loan for some time. Creditors gain, up to a point—but their apparent gains may turn to losses if their debtors are forced into bankruptcy. Bankruptcies, business failures, and the reduction of output add to the problems of the general public. If public opinion permits, governments may undertake supportive measures to alleviate the distress; if not, they may be under pressure to reduce services and eliminate programs, thus making things worse rather than better.

Paradoxical as it may sound, the last decade has vented the evils of both inflation and deflation on the economy simultaneously—and there is no end in sight. Governments not only have been deterred from introducing badly-needed measures to reduce unemployment and to support incomes, they have also been under pressure to cut back on existing social programs. The long period of too-easy money in the face of persistently-increasing inflation noted at the end of Chapter 7 led many homeowners and small businessmen (especially farmers and other primary producers) to take on obligations that suddenly became much more burdensome when interest rates were finally allowed to rise. Their problems have been compounded by the cutbacks in production that have resulted from the policies now being followed.* But the main burden has fallen on the unemployed—typically, those with least seniority and new entrants to the labour force who have no seniority at all.

It is hard to draw definitive conclusions about the net effect of this welter of conflicting factors on the distribution of income. Almost everyone can show persuasive evidence that he has been injured by the combination of inflation and deflation experienced in recent years. Wages and salaries have lagged behind prices in most countries, even for those who are still employed. Investors can also complain of hardships, however—they are taxed on their nominal returns even though their real returns are much smaller if not actually negative, they have suffered losses due to bankruptcies and defaults, and in many cases their capital values have shrunk even if none of their debtors have defaulted. Nevertheless they get important benefits from the tax shelters that are so widely available today, both for individuals and for corporations.† For these and other reasons it is clear that investors as a group have gained relative to wage- and salary-earners as a group, even though it is difficult to be more precise about the net effects in greater detail.

It should also be noted that investors enjoy an important offset to the disadvantages they suffer from the present combination of inflation and deflation. Any market interest rate contains at least three major components. One component is of course "real" or "pure" interest, the rate that would be appropriate for a risk-free loan in the absence of either inflation or deflation. Another is an inflation premium, to repay the lender for the loss of the purchasing power of the principal sum due to rising prices. Finally, there is a risk premium, to compensate for the possibility that the borrower may default. It is usually treated as zero for the debts of a responsible government, but may become appreciable even

---

* Large and middle-sized business firms have also been affected, of course, and there have been some spectacular examples of bankruptcy or threatened bankruptcy of major firms. In general, however, they have better cash flows on which to depend, they benefit from important tax advantages, and they have been able to shift much of their burdens to their suppliers and their laid-off employees. See also the third section of Chapter 11.

† Corporations are ultimately owned by individuals, and the benefits of corporate tax concessions accrue to their ultimate owners.

for such a borrower if its debts are large and growing rapidly—for markets are wary of lending too much to any one borrower, even a strong government. For other borrowers the risk premium also varies according to their individual credit ratings, and is highly sensitive to general economic conditions; not surprisingly, it rises as foreclosures and bankruptcies rise. The inflation premium and the risk premium under present conditions combine to produce the high market interest rates that burden debtors, but they provide an automatic though imperfect compensation to investors. This compensation is most easily identified in interest rates, but it tends to be reflected in all other returns to the ownership of property as well.

A Deteriorating Consensus

As noted at the end of the first section of this chapter, the acceptance of any pattern of income distribution in any society depends on a general consensus, or at the very least on an acquiescence in a compromise among differing views. A consensus emerged in Western Society after World War II that supported a substantial increase in transfer payments as some version or other of the welfare state became accepted. The new measures were typically designed to expand education and health services, to insure individuals against such misfortunes as unemployment, accident, and disease, to provide a safety net for the elderly and the disadvantaged against degrading poverty, to improve the relationship between family size and family income, or to improve on existing programs in these fields. An important consideration was that these measures would sustain aggregate demand and thus support the economy against the perceived threat of relapse into depression, in the context of the Keynesian analysis; the expanded system of transfer payments was seen not as just a drain on resources but as part of a plan for maintaining output and sharing economic misfortunes more fairly. There were of course important differences among individuals in the enthusiasm or the reluctance with which they greeted these measures, but the fact that real income was growing rapidly was undoubtedly an important factor in their acceptance: the net costs could be met largely out of the annual increase without any material decline in anyone's standard of living.

The prolonged experience of combined inflation and deflation brought on by The Fearsome Dilemma has seriously undermined the previous consensus in most countries. The contribution transfer payments make to sustaining output and employment is still as important as ever, but it is less apparent now because income has not continued to grow as expected and because the costs are rising. Unemployment-insurance benefits are now a major part of income-supporting transfers, and benefits that seemed easily sustainable when unemployment rates were expected to remain low loom much more burdensome now that double-digit rates have become common. Other costs have also escalated under the combined pressure of inflation and recession. These increases in costs are not now so easily met out of the increase in total income, and the latent disapproval by rightwing elements in the population has been aroused.

With the eclipse of demand management (temporarily, it is to be hoped), a good deal of the restiveness about transfer payments has focused on the government deficit. The rising costs of these payments are widely cited as a major cause, and there is considerable pressure to reduce them in order to reduce the deficit. However, that does not appear to be an appropriate conclusion. The qualifying conditions for income-supporting payments were set when times were good, and it may well be that in some cases they were made unduly inclusive, but the plain fact is that the increases in costs are largely due to the curtailment of output as a result of the restrictive fiscal and monetary policies currently in effect. In any case these payments are neither the only nor the most important contributors to the deficit: other major factors are high interest rates, depressed revenues from a depressed economy, and specific tax reductions.

Paralleling the rising criticisms of income-supporting transfers from those on the political right, there has been a rallying of left-of-centre elements in their defence. This polarization of opinion makes it difficult to review the present pattern of income distribution in a rational way. Furthermore the problem is likely to get worse as time goes on, unless imaginative new policy initiatives are found. The present unemployment-insurance plans in most countries were designed to support the unemployed in relatively short periods of idleness, in the expectation that they would soon find new jobs, but now many of them have been unemployed for long periods and have exhausted their entitlements. That forces them to depend on welfare payments that clearly come from grudging charity rather than from insurance funds to which they themselves have contributed and on which they have a legitimate claim, thus further reducing their incomes and at the same time hurting their pride and their self-reliance. It is doubtful that the present income-supporting system can be maintained in this unfavourable climate, let alone extended to meet the problems of long-term unemployment, without further increases in the levels of progressive taxes. This will be particularly difficult in those countries that have recently given substantial tax reductions and other favours to those in the upper income brackets.

Policy initiatives that control inflation yet permit the full use of the economy's productive capacity will greatly alleviate these problems. Even so, further measures to redistribute income will probably be called for in the future, so more of the growth in real income can be channelled to low-income groups.

Part Two

PRESCRIPTIONS

Chapter 9
A LOSING STRATEGY

Fiscal and Monetary Restraint

We have now experienced over a decade of serious world-wide inflation, and increasingly-severe measures to restrain it. The creeping inflation of the 1950's was tending to get worse everywhere in the 1960's, even in Germany and the U.S.A., and in the early 1970's there was a distinct break in the trend-line of prices in most major countries: the rate of inflation accelerated, and in most countries it accelerated greatly. Almost without exception the break came between August 1971, when the U.S.A. "temporarily" ended the convertibility of the dollar into gold or SDR's, and the end of 1973, by which time the fixed-exchange-rate system had finally collapsed and an era of fluctuating rates had begun. The annual rate of inflation reached the double-digit range in many countries by 1975, subsided temporarily, then surged upward again to record highs in 1980—in some cases to about 30 percent—before declining irregularly once more. At this writing it is down to or below 5 percent in most countries, but not all, as a result of severe countermeasures. However, there is widespread fear that any premature relaxation of present policies will risk a new upsurge of the rate.

The methods used everywhere to combat inflation have been the traditional ones of fiscal and monetary restraint—the same methods that would have been used 50 or 100 or 200 years ago. These restraints could have been made sufficiently severe to reduce inflation to zero long ago, of course, as they would have been in former times, were it not for The Fearsome Dilemma. Formerly the government's budget would have been balanced promptly and drastically, but now even the extremists do not advocate an immediate end to the deficit, and more moderate opinion seeks merely to reduce it. Demand-management techniques have not been entirely abandoned, but their scope has been severely limited. Public opinion appears to have accepted the current level of restraint, for the time being at least, as representing the best presently-available compromise between the two horns of the dilemma.

The case for the strategy of restraint has been put forcefully by Mr. de Larosière, the Managing Director of the International Monetary Fund.[1] He has urged member governments to maintain strict limits on the growth of the money supply, and to intensify their efforts to reduce or eliminate their budget deficits. He believes that this will turn the situation around and restore sustainable growth. He acknowledges that these policies explain the economic stagnation of recent years, the slump in world trade, and the plight of the developing countries that do not have oil reserves of their own. Nevertheless he argues that reversing the policies in an effort to reduce unemployment would prove mistaken: it would risk even higher rates of inflation that would in due course require even higher rates of unemployment to cure. To reduce unemployment he advocates fundamental measures to make labour costs more flexible, to make labour more easily shifted from one industry to another as conditions change, and to ensure that incentives to work are adequate.* This is of course pretty much the combination of policies being followed by most countries, under the leadership of Britain and the U.S.A., with some differences of emphasis from country to country. It is commonly identified as a monetarist solution, though monetarists are inclined to disavow some aspects at least of the policies actually being followed in their name.

Let there be no mistake about it, inflation is a very serious problem and must be vigorously combatted. Even at relatively low rates it undermines the decisionmaking process in a money-and-market economy. To give up on inflation and go all out for full employment, as some naïve critics propose, would soon bring intolerable chaos to the economy, just as unlimited spending has always done in the past. At 5 percent per annum, which many governments now seem willing to tolerate, it is still too high—about 5 percentage points too high.

However, unemployment is an equally-serious problem, for it means not only the loss of potential real output but also, more importantly, damage to human values. The current policy mix might be very different if many people in decisionmaking positions in both the private and the public sector had ever walked the streets unemployed; it is all too easy to view someone else's troubles with equanimity if you have never experienced similar problems yourself. True, we now have far better social-insurance programs and other cushioning devices than we ever had before World War II. Nevertheless the **duration** of a period of unemployment makes a great deal of difference in its effects on an individual. From the end of the war until recently, bouts of unemployment were relatively short for most of the people affected. Now, however, many victims are

---

*Mr. de Larosière apparently believes that a high rate of unemployment is a **desirable** feature of the deflationary strategy, presumably to discipline the labour force; the implication is that unreasonable wage and other demands by labour are the main cause of inflation. It does not follow that all advocates of this strategy share his views. Some may feel that high unemployment is an **undesirable** but inevitable side-effect; the implication is that demands for wage increases are not necessarily more at fault for the generation of inflation than demands for increases in other prices.

experiencing prolonged periods of unemployment. The effects are far more serious. For those who have had many years of productive and rewarding work, prolonged unemployment may so undermine their self-confidence that their work-effectiveness and therefore their employability will be seriously undermined. For school-leavers and other new entrants to the labour force, failure to learn the benefits and the discipline of productive and rewarding work experiences may adversely affect their ability to hold a job for the rest of their lives. Earlier generations had no better remedy to offer for a recession than to await the revival of private investment and hope it would lead to prosperity for a time at least, but the present generation has seen evidence that better solutions are possible.

The painful effects of the restrictive monetary and fiscal policies now being followed in the major nations are not confined to their own domestic economies, they are also visited on the developing countries. These countries are struggling to raise their standards of living by harnessing the same two forces that have been so effective elsewhere: investment in productive capital, and international trade. They hope to accomplish in a generation or two what has taken 200 years in the industrialized countries, and are relying on foreign financing and foreign technology to speed up the process. International trade is therefore doubly important to them, since it must pay for the imported capital and technology and it will let them specialize in products in which they have a comparative advantage. The world-wide recession brought on by restrictive policies in the industrialized countries to deal with their own internal problems hits the developing countries hard on both counts.

Sharp increases in interest rates and reduced levels of economic activity have had severely-adverse effects on the distribution of income in the domestic economies of the industrialized nations, as briefly noted in Chapter 8, but those effects are partly cushioned by other mechanisms. They have equally-severe effects on the international distribution of income, but in this case there is no automatic cushioning device; alleviation can only come from either voluntary concessions by the creditors, or involuntary concessions due to defaults by the debtors. This was dramatically highlighted in 1982, when a number of highly-publicized international debt crises and reschedulings intruded on public attention. The problem has since eased somewhat, thanks to some decline in interest rates from the record peaks of 1981, but it has certainly not gone away. Both sides have good reason to avoid major defaults, which would have domino effects on international financial institutions that would undoubtedly disrupt capital markets and international trade for years, as past experience amply shows.

However, the main point to note here has to do with the cause of the problem, not its solution. In some cases, it is true, improvident borrowing for dubious programs has been a factor—with the obvious corollary that there was improvident lending as well. Nevertheless most of the indebtedness was incurred to finance projects that were deemed economically viable under the circumstances envisaged by both lenders and borrowers. Those loans and those projects have not been put in jeopardy by any change in their merits as judged in terms of a sanely-operating international economic system, they have been put in jeopardy by policy initiatives taken in the industrialized countries to deal with problems that are primarily domestic. These initiatives not only drove interest rates to heights that are hard to justify, they also sharply curtailed the volume of international trade on which the developing nations must depend in order to raise their standards of living.

Two Misguided Criticisms

Two major lines of criticism are currently addressed to the economic policies being followed in most countries: that they are too severe, and that they are not severe enough. They do not cancel out, however, because they focus on different aspects of the matter. Both are mistaken. The proper criticism of these policies is that they are doomed to failure because they deal with only one aspect of the problem, as argued in the last section of this chapter. We need a strategy that will end inflation without restricting employment opportunities, and thus allow us to escape both horns of The Fearsome Dilemma.

One group of well-meaning critics says the emphasis on combatting inflation is overdone, and that we should focus more strongly on fighting unemployment even if that means higher inflation. This line of argument tacitly accepts The Fearsome Dilemma as a fact of life, and merely disputes which horn it is better to be gored by. It has become more muted since international rates of inflation have moved into and out of the double-digit range, but it is still to be heard. Some adherents advocate a deliberate depreciation of the domestic currency in order to encourage exports and discourage imports, thereby stimulating the economy. Others propose expansionary domestic policies that would not depend on export markets and would not depreciate the currency in the first instance. However, any expansion of domestic income is certain to add to import demand; it will also add to inflationary pressures and thereby make the country's exports less competitive on world markets, so currency depreciation would inevitably follow.

Unfortunately there are two major flaws in both these proposals, as past experience demonstrates. First, exchange depreciation will be seen by other countries as a deliberate effort to export unemployment and will spark retaliation in one form or another, so in the end everyone will lose and no-one will gain. Second, even if other countries acquiesce in the depreciation in a particular case (perhaps recognizing that the move is justified by special circumstances), any initial net gain will soon be vitiated by increased domestic inflation, for the reasons noted in the first section of Chapter 4. Freely-fluctuating exchange rates were widely advocated in the 1960's and 1970's, but a decade of experience has disillusioned most observers: they do not solve any problems, they merely change the symptoms. The wonder is that it has taken anyone so long to see what should have been obvious at the start.

One variant of the too-severe school of thought bypasses the question of inflation and addresses itself primarily to domestic interest rates, arguing that national policymakers in any one country should act to reduce them unilaterally. However, an interest rate is a price, as noted at the start of Chapter 1; like other prices, it has a role to play in a money-and-market economy. At any given time it may be difficult to judge what is a realistic rate of interest, but allowing the interest-rate structure to get out of line will lead to wrong decisions. (A realistic rate may be thought of as something like the "natural" rate mentioned in the last section of Chapter 7, perhaps modified in accordance with current demand-management policies). Too-low interest rates maintained for too long after World War II were undoubtedly a factor in generating the inflationary problems we now have. On the other hand the high rates reached in 1981 were probably excessive, despite the inflationary pressures of the time, and may have inflicted more damage than necessary on the world economy.

Many market rates obtaining as this is being written are about half their 1981 peaks, but may still be higher than they should be; real rates, after adjusting as best we can for inflation,* seem high by historical standards. Nevertheless there is now wide agreement among economists of various schools of thought that market interest rates in the world at large must be kept high enough to make sure they do not again subsidize inflation, and in any given country must be kept high enough

---

* The real rate of interest is commonly computed by deducting the current rate of inflation from the current level of the particular market interest rate being considered, but this is inadequate for two reasons. First, it ignores the risk-premium component in market interest rates, which is surely substantial under present conditions, though extremely difficult to measure. Second, even if the risk premium is ignored (or deemed to be included in the inflation premium), any such computation is at best a rough approximation. Quite aside from arguments about what price index should be used to measure inflation, the real interest rate for any given debt contract can only be computed with any accuracy at the end of the term, using the average rate of inflation for the entire period rather than the apparent rate at any given point in time.

to prevent destabilizing international flows of funds. Unrealistically-low domestic interest rates encourage lenders to shift their funds to external markets, and also encourage those borrowers who have a choice (like firms that operate in more than one country) to shift their borrowing to the domestic market, thus depreciating the exchange rate inappropriately.

High interest rates do impose a hardship on borrowers, particularly on homeowners with mortgages. They also are a burden to business borrowers, of course, but in this case much of the hardship attributed to them should really be attributed to the depressed state of the economy. Interest costs certainly did rise steeply in a short period of time in the early 1980's, and that attracted a lot of attention to them. Nevertheless they account for only a part of the squeeze on business profits; other costs are also pressing against profit margins, and reduced sales volumes mean that all costs must be spread over a smaller output. A successful strategy for ending inflation and restoring prosperity would thus ease the profit squeeze in three separate ways: it would reduce or eliminate both the inflation premium and the risk premium in interest rates, and it would spread all business costs over a larger volume of output and sales.

Now for the second line of criticism of current policies, the assertion that they are not severe enough. This school of thought wants to see government deficits reduced much more drastically, or eliminated entirely. They blame them for keeping market interest rates high, and argue that private investment would be stimulated if only interest rates were low enough. Not only that: they also claim that government deficits absorb funds that should go to the private sector, and thereby crowd private borrowers out of the market.

Government deficits are indeed open to valid criticisms in certain circumstances. When the economy is operating at or near capacity and employment is high, it is clear that additional government borrowing-and-spending will crowd private borrowing-and-spending out of the market, and **in those circumstances** should be limited to financing capital projects that are sound investments in themselves. But, when capital investment expenditures are insufficient to absorb the flow of savings that a fully-employed economy would generate, as is presently the case in most countries, government borrowing-and-spending can not crowd out private borrowing-and-spending that is not going to occur in any case.

Furthermore, a budget deficit when business is slack is essentially neutral with respect to interest rates. In good times and bad the money some people save must be borrowed and spent by others, or a self-reinforcing deflationary spiral like that of the 1930's will set in. The immediate effects on interest rates are not greatly different whether it is businessmen who borrow to finance new capital formation or a government that borrows to support an ailing economy.

Unfortunately, many business leaders are still ambivalent about the stabilizing role that fiscal policy can play, if not actually hostile to it. The financial community in particular is prone to focus exclusively on the heavy volume of government financing it implies. It is clear enough that, if the deficit could be eliminated **without disturbing the economy**, then interest rates would indeed be lower and debtors would be better off. However, we don't have that choice; reducing the deficit under present conditions would worsen the recession and gore us with the unemployment horn of The Fearsome Dilemma instead of the inflation horn.

The justification for keeping the interest rate as low as possible in slack times is not that it is expected to have much stimulating effect in itself, but to encourage private capital spending if and when it does begin to recover. A low interest rate **encourages but does not ensure** new capital spending. That will only occur when business sees the prospect of sufficient additional net returns from increased productive capacity to justify its cost, but in slack times the existing capacity is not fully used. New capacity will not be needed until the existing capacity is reduced by age or obsolescence, or until the economy begins to recover for some other reason (perhaps expansionist government policies).

The proper criticism for most government deficits today is not that they exist but that they benefit the wrong people. They arise partly because of automatic stabilizers (increased income-supporting expenditures and reduced revenues) triggered by restrictive fiscal and monetary policies, and partly because of specific but ineffective measures that are supposed to encourage investment and thereby revive the economy. The net result is that a large part of the deficit is due to higher interest rates, tax concessions to investment income, and reduced income-tax rates in the upper brackets, all of which benefit only the well-to-do. Relatively little of the deficit is due to income-supporting measures that benefit those who really need help.

Cumulative Deficits

The possibility of **persistent** budget deficits raises some long-run problems[2] that are not adequately dealt with in the theory of demand management as presented in Chapter 7.

In principle the government's patterns of revenue and expenditure should be such that, if private capital investment were just sufficient to absorb the flow of savings generated at the full-employment level of output, the budget would be in balance;* or perhaps that there would be a surplus designed to reduce government debts previously incurred for cyclical reasons. This is known as full-employment budgeting, and implies that **cyclical** deficits may be incurred for the support of high levels of employment. However, government deficits might become persistent for either of two reasons or some combination of them: (1) the actual patterns of government revenue and expenditure in effect over a given period of time might not produce a balanced budget even at the full-employment level of output (there might be a **structural** deficit in addition to or instead of a cyclical deficit); or (2) private capital investment might be persistently insufficient to absorb the flow of savings being generated at the current level of income, whatever that level was (cyclical deficits might become persistent).

Regardless of whether they are structural or cyclical, or to whom the debt is owed, large and persistent government deficits mean rising total indebtedness and may sooner or later face the government with difficult policy decisions. Interest costs take an increasingly large share of government expenditures and of total real output (or income), unless output is rising strongly, so the deficit feeds on itself and it becomes increasingly difficult to cover it by raising taxes or cutting expenditure. Also, the deficit is vulnerable to adverse fluctuations in interest rates. The implications are particularly obvious if any material portion of the deficit is financed directly or indirectly by borrowing abroad: the growing burden of interest payments imposes a net reduction in the real income of the domestic economy.† Even if the debt is entirely or mainly held domestically, however, rising interest costs compound the problem of income distribution, for they accrue as income to the well-to-do. At some point the fiscal burden may become so severe that a deliberate bout of inflation will appear to be the only way out; or financial markets may conclude that increased inflation is inevitable, and may refuse to accept further government issues, thus precipitating the crisis they fear.

---

*More correctly, the budget deficit would be limited to whatever was necessary to finance legitimate government capital expenditures.

†This is not true of debts incurred to finance new capital facilities, whether by the government or by private interests, provided the facilities so financed are actually put to profitable use, for the implication is that they will increase the national income by more than enough to pay for their cost. If the capital facilities are idle, however, or employed unproductively or at less than capacity, the debt service costs will be a drain on domestic income in the same way as debt incurred to finance the government's ordinary deficit. Foreign equity capital will not result in an income drain in such circumstances, since the foreign owner will receive little or no revenue, but leaves control of the enterprise in external hands.

These problems are not likely to reach serious proportions as long as the economy is maintaining a relatively high level of employment and a relatively low rate of inflation, for in those circumstances total output is likely to be growing more or less in proportion to the government's indebtedness. Under present conditions in most countries, however, the problem is already serious and threatens to get worse. Interest costs now account for a substantial and rapidly-rising portion of governmental expenditures. Unproductive government debt (i.e. debt that was not incurred to finance needed capital facilities) is large relative to real national wealth and to annual real income, and is also rising rapidly. Yet most economies are operating far below their potential levels of output, and face inflation rates that are still serious.

The logical solution to this long-term problem is to find a way out of The Fearsome Dilemma—if not along the lines suggested in Chapters 11 and 12 then by some better line of attack. That would permit the implementation of policies that would revive the economy and stimulate new capital investment, and would reduce interest rates in the process. An important side effect would be the elimination or at least the substantial reduction of cyclical budget deficits, since both interest and income-supporting costs would be reduced and revenues would be increased. If that did not reduce the government's fiscal problems to manageable proportions—if for example a structural budget deficit was evident—then some reordering of fiscal priorities would be in order. It might be found that some government expenditures could be reduced because they were excessive or wasteful or unjustified for some other reason, but it seems more likely that taxes would have to be increased. The arguments offered in Chapter 8 suggest that the costs and benefits of the various tax shelters now offered to investment income in many jurisdictions should come in for careful scrutiny.

However, the remedies favoured by most critics of government deficits are quite different: more of the same measures that have proven more effective in reducing real output and employment than in containing inflation.

Doomed to Failure

The saddest thing about the strategy advocated by Mr. de Larosière and being followed by most governments is that it is doomed to fail from the start. The all-but-universal acceptance of the strategy does not mean that there is widespread agreement among economists that it offers a satisfactory solution to our problems. Rather, it merely reflects a poverty of new ideas and insights: despite the obvious shortcomings of the restrictions, no-one has yet come up with an alternative that offers a clearly superior prospect of success without equally-serious side effects. Few economists believe that fiscal and monetary restraint will not only end inflation but also usher in a new era of prosperity and growth at stable prices. It never has and it never will. It is a reversion to the techniques of the past, which at best brought us the boom-and-bust of the business cycle and at worst gave us great depressions like that of the 1930's. It can offer little better for the 1980's.

The current strategy relies on stimulating new private capital spending as the engine of expansion, partly by reducing inflation and thereby getting interest rates down, and partly by reducing business taxes. It could only succeed if it could somehow cobble together a highly-improbable chain of events. Only the first step has been taken so far: fiscal and monetary policies have been made as restrictive as possible without provoking public revulsion. Second, the screws must be kept on until inflation has been convincingly reduced. It is clear this will take a long time yet—after several years we have at last seen some material progress, but there is still no assurance that price increases will remain low if policies are relaxed. Third, market interest rates must be reduced to a level that businessmen consider appropriately low, **and must show promise of staying there for some time.**

This third step is by no means the last of the requirements for success, nor the most important, nor the most difficult, but let us pause to note what it entails. Low market interest rates will require a sharp reduction in if not the elimination of both the inflation premium and the risk premium. Eliminating the first will be a long and painful process, as recent experience testifies, but the second will be more difficult still. The long period of economic stagnation the first implies means there will be serious risks of foreclosure or default on the debts of even the strongest and soundest business firms, let alone average or marginal firms. Risk premiums are therefore unlikely to decline materially until a business upturn is clearly under way. This combination of requirements helps to explain why restrictive fiscal and monetary policies have so much trouble getting market interest rates to go down and stay down. But note that there is another problem with this scenario: the risk premium must go down if interest rates are to go down; interest rates must go down if investment is to revive and start an economic recovery; but the recovery must begin if the risk premium is to decline.

Interest rates have indeed declined from their 1981 peaks, as has already been mentioned. However, there have been many previous periods of declining market rates since the 1950's, though the lows then recorded would have seemed high just a short time before, and were soon followed by new record highs. After a decade of restraint, both nominal and real rates still seem high by past standards; yet they now show signs of rising again instead of falling farther.

Now let us return to the difficult chain of events that must occur if the current strategy for ending inflation and restoring prosperity is to succeed. Suppose the fiscal and monetary screws are kept tight until inflation virtually disappears, market interest rates do finally decline to relatively low levels, and the economy is set for recovery. There remains a fourth requirement for success, and a critical one it is: businessmen must become confident that they can sell sufficient additional output at a fair profit to cover the cost of the new plant and equipment. In technical terms they need a positive "inducement to invest", i.e. the expected return on the investment must exceed the interest cost by some reasonable amount. Only then will the official strategy begin to succeed. No new capital spending will occur without this critical ingredient, regardless of any inducements the government may offer in the form of low interest rates, tax concessions, or even outright subsidies. But the long period of economic stagnation the three preceding steps involve means that there will probably be a great deal of underutilized productive capacity in most lines of business when the economic upturn finally comes. There will be little need for more capacity until the existing plant and equipment either wears out or is rendered obsolete by technical advances. It may therefore be some time before the rate of expansion becomes very robust.

Each step in this chain of events will be difficult to achieve in itself, let alone the complete sequence. However, against all probabilities, suppose it all does come to pass eventually, and the public patiently waits it out. Is there any assurance that the recovery will bring the economy to a high level of employment and a reasonable approximation of the full use of its productive resources? Or may we find ourselves still in a situation of chronic underemployment and continuing threats of a new recession? And what will prevent the reappearance of inflationary price increases, perhaps in the face of substantial underemployment? Just the government's threat to reimpose restrictive fiscal and monetary policies? That will do little to encourage the stable rate of new capital formation necessary to support continued prosperity.

Doesn't this all sound distressingly like a return to the boom-and-bust cycle of the 19th and early 20th centuries, which ended in The Great Depression of the 1930's?

It is of course possible that the authorities will relax their restrictive policies before they have had their desired effect in full, despite Mr. de

Larosière's warning that so doing will merely generate more trouble in the future. The U.S. economy is even now experiencing a recovery from its recent low point, though interest rates are still relatively high (certainly high enough to draw vigourous complaints from other countries) and the rate of inflation also remains disappointingly high. Perhaps the authorities feel they must bend their own rules a bit, at least until the 1984 presidential election is over. How long into the new presidential term will it be before the screws will have to be tightened once more?

Chapter 10
OTHER INEFFECTIVE REMEDIES

Essentials for Success

The argument of this book may be summed up in three points:

(1) Today's inflation arises and persists because our modern money-and-market-plus-demand-management system does not include a reliable and satisfactory mechanism for ensuring that "tomorrow's" money income is enough, and just enough, to buy the net total real output at "today's" prices. Individual money incomes are freely determined by the market mechanism, but the overall total escapes effective control.

(2) In principle, the authorities have ample power to limit the spending stream to any amount they deem necessary to squeeze out inflation. In practice, however, they can not use their powers effectively without raising unemployment to intolerable levels.

(3) Even if the traditional disinflationary policies now being followed all-but-universally in the world economy could be pressed with sufficient vigour to end inflation, it would not ensure a satisfactory recovery of output and employment.

The only way to escape this dilemma, and yet retain the benefits of a money-and-market economy, is to find some means of tailoring money income to real income at stable prices. That will permit demand-management techniques to be used to maintain output and employment at close to their potential levels. However, that in itself will not be enough; in addition, whatever measure or combination of measures is used to control inflation must be seen to be fair to all concerned. Inflation has been gathering momentum since World War II, its actual and anticipated effects have become deeply entrenched, and we must all share the blame. Curing it will be painful as well as difficult: those pains must be equitably shared. That means the strategy must be acceptable to the majority of the population. As a practical matter it also means it must be acceptable to all or most major sectors and influential groups, such as business in general, small business in particular, labour, farmers, fishermen, homeowners, or renters.

In searching for a strategy that will meet these two requirements, we must acknowledge that some price movements are **functional**, as noted in the first section of Chapter 1; in themselves they are neither inflationary nor deflationary, they merely reflect the role of the price mechanism in reallocating economic resources as conditions change. A good example would be higher costs for minerals due to the depletion of higher-grade ores, or the need to extend the production of certain raw materials to more-remote sources of supply. Another example would be higher costs of important imports, or the need to substitute previously-higher-priced alternatives for them, as in the case of the sharp increases in energy costs after the 1974 upsurge in oil prices. Such price increases represent unavoidable reductions in the real income of the community as a whole, and should be fairly shared by all. They should therefore be excluded from any price index used for computing cost-of-living adjustments in pensions, social benefits, income-tax exemptions, and the like, as well as in wages under collective bargaining agreements.

Resolute insistence by any strong group on maintaining its former real income in such circumstances, or rigid adherence to contractual or customary linkages of income adjustments to price movements (however well justified in normal circumstances), could easily set the price-cost spiral spinning dizzily upwards; for a concrete example, look at the effects of linking wages to the exchange rate during the German inflation of 1923, described in Chapter 2. Surely, however, such speculation is quite unnecessary and irrelevant. The excess of enforceable claims to "tomorrow's" money income over the value of current output at current prices does not come from power-plays by arrogant special-interest groups, but from the simple summation of many individual bargains and decisions, each of which appears quite feasible in itself but ignores the combined effect on the spending stream. The problem is how to control these individually-small but collectively-great effects in the price-setting process.

We must also recognize that our expectations have escalated at the same time as inflation, and ask ourselves whether they are fully justified. Despite the disappointments of the last decade or so, we continue to think that a substantial rate of growth of economic output and of everyone's real income is normal. However, the gap between the living standards in the industrialized countries and in the developing countries raises the question of whether residents of the former are entitled to add indefinitely to their already-high real incomes, if they thereby pre-empt the use of natural resources that might better be used for the benefit of residents of the latter. There is a group of thoughtful scientists who believe the growth of the world's real income must end fairly soon, perhaps early in the 21st century, because of the finite limits on its resources. (The rapid growth of the world's population is of course an additional complicating factor.) If their analysis proves to be right, then the basis of economic policymaking in all countries will have to be drastically revised. Whether they are right or wrong, however, it is highly doubtful that the world's productive capacity could support raising the world's standard of living to that already obtaining in the industrialized countries. These considerations are far beyond the scope of this book, but they indicate that sorting out our legitimate from our illegitimate expectations will complicate the task of eliminating inflation.

Monetarist and Similar Proposals

Monetarist proposals have already entered the discussion at several points. The anti-inflation strategy being followed in most countries is in general similar to monetarist prescriptions, even though monetarists do not necessarily accept them as proper applications of their doctrines, so most of the criticisms in Chapter 9 apply to them also. Nevertheless some additional comments may be in order.

To recapitulate, Friedman's prescriptions include not only a strict limit on the growth of the money supply but also a sharp reduction in or the elimination of many government transfer payments and of its economic interventions in general. His solution for The Fearsome Dilemma is to focus primarily on ending inflation, and to allow "natural" forces to reduce unemployment to its "natural" level (if indeed it could ever depart from it), i.e. unemployment would be solely voluntary. Evidently the public should accept whatever distribution of real income is brought about "naturally" in the process.

The ultimate success of these prescriptions, if they were ever applied in full, would depend on the answers to three questions: (1) Would the monetarist predictions be realized in practice? (2) How long would it take to achieve success or to demonstrate failure? (3) Would the general public accept the distribution of real income that would result?

On the first point, we have already argued in Chapter 9 that the answer is no. *Laissez-faire* policies never brought sustained prosperity at stable prices in the past, and won't do so now.

On the second point, most critics would surely agree that, even if the success of monetarist policies were indeed assured eventually, the waiting time would be intolerably long. The Great Depression engulfed the world for the decade before World War II, and the British economy was stagnant for half a decade before that, while *laissez-faire* policies by and large held sway. (The main exception was the unsuccessful effort of central banks to manage prices by means of the money supply.) It is true that those difficulties were intensified by what we now see to have been mistaken policies, as noted in the first section of Chapter 7, but "natural" restorative forces proved disappointingly slow, to say the least; and many earlier experiences, though for the most part less traumatic, led to the same conclusion. The history of the fiscal and monetary restraints imposed in many countries since 1975, more or less as proposed by monetarists, suggest that the process will be no more rapid nowadays.

On the third point, the essence of the *laissez-faire* remedy for depression and unemployment is for real wages to decline until the costs of production fall far enough to make new investment in productive capacity profitable again. To be blunt about it, this process means starving workers into cut-throat competition for existing jobs. Falling wages and falling prices produce what is technically known as the "cash balances effect" or the "wealth effect": they continually raise the real value or purchasing power of a given stock of money, so holders of money and other financial assets feel increasingly wealthy; nominal and real interest rates fall, just as they normally do if the money supply is increased while prices remain constant, since the value of the money stock relative to the value of real output changes similarly in both cases; at some point investors find it profitable to start new capital expenditure projects. Unfortunately, declining wages mean a declining spending stream, so total sales (and total output) may have to fall pretty low before recovery begins.

The implications for income distribution are obvious. Declining real wages mean that labour gets a declining part of total real output even if no involuntary unemployment occurs, and the owners of productive resources get more. Shades of Karl Marx, who talked of capitalism creating a reserve army of the unemployed and predicted the increasing misery of the proletariat! If that process went very far or lasted very long, would revolution be far behind? Are monetarists really prepared to contemplate that possibility?

As noted in section 7 of the Appendix, monetarist belief in *laissez faire* is shared by several other schools of thought. They differ on certain points of doctrine, but their prescriptions are broadly similar. Advocates of "supply-side" economics are one such group. Their name suggests that the attack on inflation will be aimed at raising the output of goods and services available to the consumer, presumably by reducing costs or increasing productivity or improving work incentives, rather than by reducing demand. That would indeed be helpful; the real question is how is it to be done, and at what cost to other policy objectives. However, most supply-siders seem to be looking rather narrowly at the government sector, seeking to reduce both government spending and taxes. The argument is that taxes are so high as to be counterproductive, and that lower tax **rates** would actually produce more tax **revenues** because they would restore work incentives. Government spending is to be reduced, partly by cutting down on social security and other transfer payments and partly by reducing government controls over business. The budget is to be balanced, or brought more nearly into balance, thereby releasing market funds to finance private investment and increased employment. The phased reduction of taxes in the U.S.A. by President Reagan early in his administration was a direct application of this philosophy, but it helped to increase the government's deficit instead of reduce it.

Price and Wage Controls

The simplest and most direct proposal for controlling inflation, and superficially an attractive one, is price and wage controls. As noted at the end of the second section of Chapter 7, it would indeed permit the price and the quantity components of the spending stream to be treated separately—**if** the controls could be made really effective and **if** they did not create new problems of their own. Unfortunately, these conditions are hard to fulfill.

Past experience with controls in many countries at many times has pretty well discredited them in the eyes of the public. Even in wartime, when patriotism could be expected to modify normal market responses to some extent, they proved difficult to apply effectively. In some peacetime applications their unsatisfactory performance was partly due to technical faults in the measures employed: as a rule they were not supported by appropriate complementary policies, they were introduced as merely temporary measures from the start, and any restraining effects they had initially were vitiated by a subsequent surge of catch-up increases. In some cases they were used as a device for suppressing the inflationary effects of an inappropriate growth of the money supply, which in turn was part of the mistaken policy of maintaining unduly-low interest rates, so it was easy to see they would fail before long: price-setters just bided their time. In most cases the enforcement mechanism was weak or lacking altogether; sometimes the program consisted of mere guidelines and moral suasion.

Technical faults are only part of the story, however; evidently it is extremely difficult for a program of controls to be seen as fair to all parties. The Canadian anti-inflation program of 1975-78 was better conceived than most, was at least moderately successful in attaining its announced goals, and was not followed by any significant catch-up increases, yet its demise was widely welcomed. It was supported by fiscal restraint, by a monetary policy that promised (and delivered) a progressive reduction in the rate of growth of the money supply to reduce inflationary expectations, and by a vigourous effort to enlist the coöperation of business, labour, provincial governments, and other interests. It included specific targets for wage and salary increases, guidelines for profits, rents, and professional fees, and measures addressed to certain structural problems. Nevertheless it proved impossible to persuade all parties that they were being treated fairly. Businessmen and provincial governments generally approved the program, though they questioned or disagreed with some aspects of it. Organized labour on the other hand was strongly and vociferously opposed; its leaders alleged that is was directed mainly at wages and would have little effect on prices. The control of profits proved difficult, predictably, so the public's sense of fairness was offended; yet the profit guidelines may have blunted investment incentives.

Even if a consensus could be achieved on a system of price and wage controls that was considered reasonably fair to all, there would be severe administrative problems to be overcome. The price structure in a modern money-and-market economy is an incredible maze of interrelated figures, as raw materials, partly-processed goods, finished goods, and services are bought and sold and resold many times before the final product lands in the hands of the ultimate consumer. An obvious example is purchases and sales among the various stages in the production of a single product, say foodstuffs moving from the farm to the processor to the wholesaler to the retailer to the consumer. However, transactions occur at each stage with various stages of other lines of production. To take the case of foodstuffs again, the farmer's inputs are not limited to seed and his own labour, they include fertilizer, rent, interest, and the services of expensive machinery, all bought from other productive processes; even the seed is not likely saved out of the previous crop, but may be a registered hybrid variety purchased from a specialist, and his own food may be bought rather than homegrown. And of course the same sort of thing occurs at every stage in every productive process. Trying to monitor costs, profits, and prices in all these transactions is a Herculean task.

In any case there is an anomoly in thus linking controls over **wages** and **prices**. Wages are prices too—the prices of various labour services. But, as noted several times already, they constitute a special kind of prices: factor returns. The other similar set of prices is factor returns to ownership. Under reasonably competitive conditions without controls, individual wages (i.e. personal remuneration of all kinds) and individual rents, interest rates, and other returns to ownership are set solely by the interaction of market forces. Now suppose inflationary pressures make themselves felt, controls are placed on all prices except factor returns, and for the sake of argument let us suppose that this Herculean task is accomplished with complete success. Market forces will still determine the **relative** values of all factor returns, and there is nothing in these assumptions to suggest they will be any different from what they would be without the controls (they will all be less in absolute terms because of the controls, but presumably the percentage reductions will be the same). By hypothesis the inflation will be ended, and all factors of production will be as well off as before.

However, that is not the way controls are usually imposed: they are set independently for wages and for intermediate and final prices, i.e. on all prices **except** returns to the ownership of productive capital. Wages will then be constrained by the general limitation on intermediate and final prices **and** by the specific limit on wages, other factor returns will be constrained only by the general limitation; market forces will operate within those constraints. Wages can be monitored by direct comparison with the standard laid down, other factor returns can be monitored only on a transaction-by-transaction basis through the market system. Wages will thus be set by a dual standard within the overall controls, *ex cathedra et ex foro*, i.e. by authority and by the market, whereas other factor returns will be set *ex foro* alone. If there is any slack in the system of controls, the benefit will certainly go to the owners of productive resources.

But we are still not by any means finished with the problems associated with price and wage controls. Despite the difficulties already recited, suppose not only that a consensus is achieved on a set of price and wage controls that the public accepts as reasonable under the circumstances, but also that the administrative problems are fully overcome. Experience indicates this will interfere in various ways with the efficiency of the pricing system in regulating decisionmaking in the economy; probably the most obvious features will be shortages of certain goods, line-ups, under-the-counter deals that channel scarce goods to favoured customers, grey or black markets, and so on. Never mind all that—perhaps the public will accept these developments philosophically, feeling that they are better than unfettered inflation. The question is, **will the controls end inflation?** Probably not, for reasons that go to the root of the free-enterprise system.

Recall the discussion of "profit" in the broad sense and "pure profit" in the economist's sense in the fourth section of Chapter 3. You could hardly expect the public to accept a limit on wages, salaries, and the like without equivalent limits on profits in the broad sense. What does that mean for pure profit? Well, it is one thing to identify the **concept** of pure profit as explained in an academic textbook, but it is quite another to identify the **actuality** in the real world. If you look at the financial statements of a corporation, how can you tell how much of its reported profit is a normal return to invested capital, how much is a monopolistic profit due to market advantages, how much is a mere windfall profit, and how much is a pure profit? For the purpose of enforceable price control, profit would have to be defined in standard accounting terms. The prospects of being able to exempt pure profit would be pretty poor.

You may well question how effective an incentive the hope of a pure profit really is in a world of imperfect or monopolistic competition; nevertheless it is the one factor in the money-and-market system that tends to induce efficient productive techniques and to pass the benefits on to the consumer in the form of lower prices. But, if business enterprises were required to limit their profits, nothing could be simpler: all they would need to do is to stop trying to devise more cost-efficient techniques. Time and money so spent would be wasted, since they would produce no benefits. Everyone would be entitled to pass on any costs he had incurred, plus the prescribed markup. The results would be **cost-plus** inflation.* The authorities would still have to validate whatever rate of price increase the economy happened to generate, or see unemployment rise.

And what would regulate the rate of price increase the economy would generate? For that matter, what regulates it now? Well, clearly no seller can afford to get too far out of step with his nearest competitors, so that at least puts some restraint on the rate at which inflation can accelerate; but there seems to be no obvious ceiling on the rate of inflation itself. Every now and then we may expect the public to become so upset with the current rate that it will countenance pretty drastic countermeasures, which should slow the process down for a while, but what is to stop it gradually accelerating again thereafter?

Incomes Policies

So-called "incomes policies" sound as if they should be addressed specifically to keeping money income and real income in step, but in practice they are addressed primarily (in some cases exclusively) to wages, salaries, and other forms of personal remuneration. This is analytically

---

* Do you remember the joke about the three businessmen who met for lunch during World War II? The first reached for the bill and offered to pay for all three; "I can put it on my expense account, and I'll get 50 percent back on my corporate income tax." "Oh no!" said the second, "Let me have it! I am in the excess-profit-tax bracket, I'll get 85 percent of it back!" "No indeed, I'll take it" said the third, "I'm on a cost-plus-contract—I'll make money on it!"

unsound as well as unfair. It is analytically unsound, because it treats only one category of factor costs and ignores the second, which accounts for 30 percent or so of net national income in a typical modern economy. It is unfair, because it exempts a major income-category from any of the burdens that restraining inflation will inevitably entail. If one participant in a joint productive process exercises restraint in claiming a share of the output and the other does not, it is easy to see who will benefit the most. An incomes policy that would meet these objections would have to cover all factor returns to the ownership of property—rents, interest, dividends, retained profits, capital gains, and all—as well as personal emoluments. Like price controls, that would eliminate pure profits and their role in promoting cost-efficient productive techniques.

One variant, a "tax-based incomes policy" (TIP), has attracted considerable support in academic circles.[1] The idea is to give a tax-inducement to producers to keep costs down, either by a tax penalty for exceeding certain guidelines or by a tax reduction for keeping within them. An interesting procedural aspect is that it is commonly proposed to apply the plan only to the largest firms—in the U.S.A. it is estimated that the 2000 largest businesses account for 85 percent of total business output, and it is usually suggested that a TIP need apply only to them. It is further argued that calculating the tax will require only about seven additional lines on the corporate income-tax return, so the administrative costs would be relatively small. Government employees would be held to wage increases at some standard guideline rate, with catch-up adjustments every few years if they lagged behind the private sector. Supplementary provisions might be devised for important activities like trucking and construction, where small firms predominate, and for other special cases.

Critics of the TIP have argued that it would be ineffective if not actually counterproductive. They suggest that, if the tax were less than 100 percent of the increase in selling prices, the firm might simply factor it into its price structure; the net effect would be to accelerate inflation instead of reduce it. If only a part of the price increase could be passed on to the purchaser, the acceleration of inflation would be less; but, even if none of the tax could be shifted, inflation might remain unabated.

Also, TIP's would be vulnerable to substitution effects and problems of quality control. For example, substituting less-skilled and cheaper forms of labour might reduce labour costs to the detriment of quality; expanding the output of higher-markup "quality" goods with little increase in labour costs and reducing the availability of standard-quality goods would increase profits without attracting much if any more tax; and more capital-intensive methods might be used to reduce the wage bill and thus reduce the tax liability. All these manoeuvres would generate disguised price increases. In addition the TIP penalty would apply impartially against functional price increases as well as merely inflationary price increases, thus interfering with the rational allocation of productive resources to industries facing rising real costs for legitimate reasons.

Some TIP's are addressed solely to wage costs and other forms of personal remuneration, in which case the tax could be avoided by subcontracting work to small exempt firms. The plan should therefore be addressed to all costs, including purchases of materials and services and capital-cost allowances. In any case, however, the returns to the ownership of productive resources and the remuneration of management and executives seem most likely to be able to escape the impact of a TIP; the net burden on the firm, after deducting whatever portion could be shifted to customers, would fall in its full rigour on the rank and file of wage-earners.

A final criticism, perhaps the most serious of all, is that no version of the TIP offers any assurance that the total of "tomorrow's" enforceable money-income claims will be compatible with "tomorrow's" output valued at "today's" prices.

The Market Anti-Inflation Plan

A proposal called the Market Anti-Inflation Plan (MAP) is designed to operate directly on both wages and profits and uses the market mechanism to achieve an equilibrium position.[2] It would permit the money supply to be increased by just the amount necessary for economic health, instead of by whatever amount is needed to validate as much of the sum of independently-determined money-income claims as is necessary to keep unemployment within tolerable bounds, and to stabilize average prices while leaving individual prices and wages free to adjust to changing circumstances. The idea is to offer a strong market-determined incentive to all firms to limit any increases in their net sales per unit of input of productive resources, and to use the market mechanism to equate the increase in total net sales for the nation with the increase in real output. (Net sales means value added, and equals the sum of profits and wages—i.e., factor costs. For government enterprises and nonprofit organizations it becomes "individual incomes generated.")

As envisaged for the U.S.A., the proposal requires the Federal Reserve System (i.e. the central bank) to set up a MAP-Credit Office and to open accounts for all firms, crediting each with 100 percent of the previous year's net sales plus the estimated increase in productivity. Hiring an additional employee will give the firm an additional credit equal to his wage in his previous employment; releasing an employee will cost it credit equal to his wage. Similarly, the addition or liquidation of capital will add to or reduce the firm's MAP-credit balance. Net sales in excess of its credit balance require it to buy equivalent credit from other firms; net sales that fall short of its credit balance permit it to sell the unused credit to other firms. The MAP-Credit Office will be charged with setting up a free market in these credits.

Suppose inflation is running at 10 percent per annum when the plan is introduced, the average national increase in productivity is estimated to be 2 percent per annum, and a typical firm plans to add 2 percent to its input of labour and capital services during the year: the firm's net sales in current dollars would be increasing by 14 percent per annum. Now the authorities announce that net sales for the economy will be allowed to increase by only 4 percent in the coming year (2 percent for productivity and 2 percent for new inputs), or just enough to cover the expected increase in real output at current prices. A typical firm may at first attempt to buy an additional 10 percent of MAP credits, and may be prepared to pay a stiff price for them in the expectation of passing on these costs to its customers. As it becomes apparent that the actual increase in total net sales for the economy will in fact be limited to 4 percent, however, the expectation of higher selling prices will diminish, and so will the demand for excess MAP credits; when inflation and inflationary expectations cease, the price of MAP credit should fall to zero.

The proponents of the MAP recognize that it could not be successfully introduced unless the public became convinced that it would end or at least reduce inflation. Given this acceptance, they believe it could end inflation very quickly—so quickly that it might be necessary for the government to arbitrarily intervene to abrogate or modify certain contractual arrangements based on the expectation of continuing inflation, much as the U.S. government in 1934 abrogated the gold clauses then found in many contracts, after the official price of gold was raised from $20.67 to $35.00 per ounce. Alternatively, the MAP could be introduced gradually over a period of years; each firm could be granted additional MAP credits equal to say 80 percent of the current inflation rate the first year, 60 percent the second, and so on.

It is clear that a great many practical questions will have to be answered before any attempt could be made to put the MAP into effect. Meanwhile critics raise questions about its administrative feasibility and about how to enforce compliance on the part of business and labour. They estimate that an application in the U.S.A. would involve 13-

million firms, in contrast to only about 2000 firms for the TIP. However, there would seem to be no reason why the MAP could not use the same device as the TIP, i.e. limit the program to a relatively small number of the largest firms. That would enormously reduce the administrative problems, and the wage-and-price leadership of these powerful firms should pretty well ensure that smaller firms would comply reasonably satisfactorily. If necessary, the program could be gradually extended to medium-sized and smaller firms.

Surely the most serious fault of the MAP is that (like the TIP) it would destroy the functional role of pure profits as the incentive to innovate and to allocate productive resources efficiently, which is a major virtue of the free-enterprise system. Higher-than-average net sales per unit of input may of course be due to the exercise of naked market power, which certainly needs to be curtailed in the public interest just as much as inflation itself, but it may also be due to the earning of a pure profit by reason of either cost-reducing innovations within the firm or a shift in market demand towards a particular industry or product; in the latter case the proper response of the market system is to direct more resources toward the industry or firm producing the product concerned. Firms or industries with below-average net sales, on the other hand, will presumably be those that are relatively inefficient or are losing favour with the consuming public. The MAP would penalize expanding firms and industries by scooping out their pure profit to pay for extra MAP credits, and subsidize stagnant or declining firms and industries by offering them a market for their unusable MAP credits and by encouraging them to retain redundant workers lest they lose equivalent credit.

Evaluation

This concludes the description of all the serious proposals I know of for dealing with inflation, and inferentially with The Fearsome Dilemma. As you can see, my evaluation of them is essentially negative: only the MAP attempts to tailor money income to real income; none of them clearly addresses the question of fairness to all sectors of the economy; and the MAP, while promising in some respects, may not prove administratively feasible.

However, my assessment is not by any means completely negative. In some cases it is more a matter of skepticism about practical applications, or a Scotch verdict of "not proven" rather than an outright "no". And some positive comments may certainly be added. A reduction in the rate of growth of the money supply, as advocated by monetarists, must play a part in any remedy for inflation. The TIP proposals point to interesting possibilities in the use of taxation, quite aside from their specific measures: perhaps business taxes should be addressed to costs instead of profit or income. That would give firms a double incentive for economizing, since so doing would reduce their tax base as well as add to their pretax profits. The proposers of the MAP should be applauded for their efforts to find a set of market-oriented incentives to curtail inflation. Perhaps some or all of these proposals will find a part in the final solution.

Chapter 11
A WINNING STRATEGY

Towards a Permanent Solution

In Chapter 5 it was argued that the roots of inflation lie in the price-setting process, and that curing it will involve a revival of microeconomics. Just how this is to be done is presently far from clear, but it is not likely that it can be done quickly or easily. The problem has been building up since the early 1950's, while the public's attitudes and expectations have hardened into patterns that may prove very difficult to change—patterns of materialism, patterns of self-interest, patterns of confrontation and intransigeance, all based on the confident expectation of ever-growing real income.

Some way must be found to introduce the interests of the general public into all or most price decisions, through a third party besides the buyers and the sellers immediately concerned: some way of ensuring that the two principals recognize and take due account of the externalities of their actions, and of making the overall result consistent with the best interests of the economy as a whole. At any point in time the maximum sustainable real output is essentially a fixed and determinate figure, which can only be increased over time as new productive facilities and new technology permit. It seems inevitable that there will be some degree of conflict among the various participants in the productive process with respect to how the total output should be divided, but surely we can find some way of solving that conflict that neither sacrifices some of the potential output and produces unnecessary unemployment nor involves the systematic encouragement of inflation.

How can we do it?

Representing the public interest on a meaningful scale will involve direct participation in major spending and pricing decisions, not merely admonitions in advance or a review of decisions after the event. These decisions will have major effects on the profitability of particular projects and firms, on resource allocation, on production and productive efficiency, on incomes and income distribution, and on many other sensitive matters. Account must be taken of the various costs involved, alternative production techniques, the costs and prices of competing goods, and all the complexities of domestic and world markets. It will obviously be extremely difficult to make the public's participation in this process effective without introducing intolerable confusion and delay.

Coöperation from agriculture, from labour, from business, and from all important special-interest groups will be essential.

It seems probable that bringing the pricing process under effective control will involve some increase in government intervention in the economy, because the government is the principal body that can take a community-wide viewpoint. However, this intervention will have to take a more flexible and imaginative form than any program of price and wage controls yet devised, and will have to be more binding than mere guidelines.

Nor will it do to simply hand the problem over to the government and hope for the best. The theory of government has to some extent evolved and must further evolve in parallel with the changes that have occurred in economic theory. Even the most democratically elected of governments can not pretend to act as the dutiful servant of the electorate, listening passively to what the public says it wants and how much it is willing to pay, then conscientiously seeking the point of indifference at the margin between those demands and the corresponding costs. That would be the political equivalent of the model of perfect competition in economics, whereas the model of imperfect or monopolistic competition offers a more realistic pattern. Just like any business firm choosing its products and its selling prices, a political party that hopes to win or retain power must put together a package of spending and taxing measures the political leaders think will appeal to the public, then enlist the wiles of the public-relations fraternity to sell it to the electorate. The pricing decisions of government as well as those of business enterprises need monitoring in the public interest.

In any case it must be acknowledged that governments and the regulatory bodies they set up are obvious targets for lobbying by the interests they are supposed to control. Much of this is quite legitimate, of course, for regulators must take due account of the practical realities in the fields subject to their control, and much of their information must come from those being regulated. Nevertheless it may be difficult for the regulators to keep the special interests of a particular industry or other economic group and the general interest of the public at large in proper perspective. It would therefore seem wiser to delegate the monitoring of prices to an independent body that would be primarily concerned with the pricing process throughout the economy.

Some years ago a certain labour leader in the North American automobile industry, in the midst of acrimonious negotiations for a new wage contract, proposed that representatives of labour **and representatives of consumers** take part in setting auto prices, and that the union should be prepared to moderate its wage demands in return. So far nothing concrete has come of it: other labour leaders and management have both shown acute disinterest. Just how useful such an arrangement would be would depend largely on how deeply the representatives of consumers were allowed to become involved in the internal affairs of the companies with which they were concerned, and how imaginatively they were able to approach their tasks. At one extreme the experiment might prove merely an exercise in tokenism. At another extreme it might become nothing but a source of obstruction. Yet skillful and well-informed delegates of the public interest, if they could win the real coöperation of labour and management, might make a major contribution to controlling inflation.

A capable and independent consumers' association with adequate research capability and assured access to the business records of at least the major producers might successfully represent the interests of the general public as a participant in the pricing process. The role of the consumer, after all, is common to all members of society. Consumers' associations are to be found in several countries; at present their interest is largely focused on comparing the relative values offered by competing brands of goods at prices encountered at typical retail outlets, and their resources are rather limited, but they have built up competent research staffs and have won a reputation for integrity. They have already broadened their interests to include service industries to some extent. One possibility is that governments might be persuaded to delegate increased responsibility to these associations and to provide them with additional funds, thereby permitting them to extend their activities to cover the productive process itself as well as the testing and comparing of finished products, and to extend their coverage of services.

Immediate Measures

We can not afford to wait patiently for a perfect solution, nor can we just throw up our hands in the face of The Fearsome Dilemma. We can't afford high unemployment with its attendant evils at home and abroad, nor inflation at even the rate of 5 percent per annum most governments now seem willing to tolerate, which wipes out about 28 percent of capital values every five years. Despite the lack of agreement among economists about the ultimate causes of inflation, there is sufficient common ground to support a pragmatic approach that should appeal to all who are more concerned with finding a solution to the problem than with defending the tenets of some economic theology or other.

Focusing on factor costs or factor returns offers a winning strategy. It will permit money income to be tailored to real output without adverse pressure on employment. It will be basically fair, because all income will be treated equivalently. Factor returns are readily identifiable in the hands of the receivers, and can be monitored without having to track down all costs and markups through the maze of intermediate and final transactions.

A successful anti-inflation strategy certainly must include restraint on nominal wages, salaries, and all other forms of personal remuneration. Just what form it should take need not be spelled out at this stage, and indeed it would be presumptuous to attempt to do so; many complicated issues are involved that will have to be carefully considered in order to ensure that all groups and categories are treated as fairly as possible, and there is a substantial body of past experience in the field that needs to be taken into account. The essential point is that increases in the total wage and salary bill of the economy must be kept in step with increases in real output. As a practical matter wage rates for (say) the coming year might be set in terms of an arbitrarily-chosen base year, adjusted as necessary to correct obvious anomolies. (For example, wage rates last corrected for the increase in the cost of living early in the base year might need topping up compared to others negotiated late in the year.) The total wage bill in the new year would then only increase as total output increased.

The major challenge will be to devise a comparable restraint on returns to the ownership of resources, in a form that will not prejudice the search for pure profits, for there are few precedents here. What we need is a levy on all nominal investment returns, designed to reduce them in the same proportion as nominal wages and salaries are reduced by whatever restraints are imposed on personal remuneration. Let's call it an Investment Levy. It should come "off the top" of all property income, tangible and intangible, just as a wage restraint will come "off the top" of the nominal wages that would otherwise be payable, and the remainder should be subject to normal income-tax.

As a practical matter the Investment Levy might be applied as an interest-rate adjustment, on the arbitrary assumption that all property returns include an implicit interest component. For property not yielding an immediate return, such as some types held for capital gains, it should be applied as a minor capital levy in order to ensure that it was collected in those cases too. It should be addressed to property income in the hands of those who ultimately benefit from it, so businesses would not treat it as a cost. Nevertheless it could be collected through the payers of interest and other returns to property (especially through business firms) as a withholding tax, like the withholding tax on wages and salaries, to minimize evasion.

To take a simple numerical example, suppose inflation is running at 5 percent per annum and a readily-identifiable typical interest rate stands at about 10 percent per annum when the new strategy is introduced. (These figures are chosen just to simplify the arithmetic.) Some form of wage and salary restraint would be applied, to hold nominal wages in the coming year about 5 percent less than would otherwise be the case. At the same time an Investment Levy of a flat 0.5 percentage points (i.e. 5 percent of 10) would be deducted from all actual or imputed returns to capital property. However, if at the end of the year it turned out that nominal wage increases were above the target level, or if the chosen interest rate had fallen (as it probably would if the strategy was successful in reducing inflation), then a proportionate part of the Investment Levy would be refunded (probably as an income-tax credit in most cases). New targets would be set each year for wages and for the Investment Levy.

Thus a combination of a well-designed program of wage restraints and an Investment Levy should quickly bring the sum of all money incomes into line with current real income at stable prices, and thereby solve The Fearsome Dilemma. Demand-management techniques would again be free to pursue high levels of output and employment. Individuals would remain free to increase their personal incomes by extra effort or by innovative ingenuity. Interest rates should decline to some extent quite promptly, because monetary and fiscal restraint would no longer have to bear all the burden of fighting inflation; and further declines should occur as the inflation premium disappeared and the risk premium declined.

The Investment Levy is the only real novelty in this proposed strategy. However, there are good reasons why investors should be prepared to accept it as part of a comprehensive plan. For one thing, while they presently enjoy some degree of inflation protection in the form of historically-high nominal interest rates and other returns, those rates and returns are highly volatile—instruments that yielded 15 to 20 percent in 1981 are yielding half that in the early months of 1984. Second, these rates include not only an inflation premium but also a substantial though uncertain risk premium, as already argued. The first should decline if inflation falls farther and the second if prosperity returns, which is exactly what this strategy is designed to accomplish; and investors would surely be glad to relinquish both in exchange for an end to the uncertainties that give rise to them. Finally, the Investment Levy would automatically decline and expire with inflation. Hence investors are not asked to make much of a sacrifice, and can expect a substantial reward.

It may be noted that there is a precedent of sorts for the strategy here proposed. Back in 1925, when Britain returned to the gold standard at what many people thought was too high a parity for the pound (i.e. at the pre-1914 parity, "so the pound could look the dollar in the face"), the late J.M. Keynes made a proposal. He had opposed the move, but suggested that the problem could be materially eased by a simple agreement between the government and the trade unions. He proposed asking the trade unions to accept an immediate reduction of, say, 5 percent in **money** wages, reversible in due course if the cost of living failed to fall by the same amount and thus restore their **real** wages. He supposed the unions would then want to know what would happen to rents, profits, and interest—the very question the Investment Levy is designed to answer. The reply he suggested was "the very rough-and-ready expedient of levying an additional income tax" of the same 5 percent on all incomes other than from employment, until real wages recovered.[1] Thus he, too, focused on factor returns as a means of controlling prices, and offered a remedy quite similar to the strategy here proposed. Unfortunately, his suggestion was not acted upon. Had something like that been done, the subsequent history of Britain and the world might have been far less painful.

Transitional Measures

Measures as far-reaching as those just proposed should not be introduced at a single stroke, however. Much explanation and persuasion would be necessary before everyone could be expected to accept them as sufficiently fair, and it would no doubt take a good deal of time to work out the details. Organized labour would want to be sure its legitimate bargaining rights would be protected, and that business profits would really be effectively restrained. Management would want to be sure the market mechanism would not be interfered with, and that the limitations on labour costs would hold. Various categories of investors would need to be persuaded they were being fairly treated—for example, bondholders and equityholders might perceive their interests differently. No-one would want to be the first to commit himself. It would probably be necessary, therefore, to put an immediate but temporary freeze on all prices and wages while all these matters were threshed out. It might also be necessary to impose a temporary tax on windfall profits in order to get the coöperation of labour (and perhaps bondholders too), since the re-expansion of output this strategy envisages would probably boost equity earnings disproportionately.* Such measures would not cause

---

* Overhead costs would presumably be covered already at the initial level of output, and the increase in revenue as sales increased would materially exceed the increase in variable costs.

any serious new distortions in the economy, however, as long as they did not last too long.

Another transitional measure might be some form of interest-rate relief in certain cases, particularly for some homeowners and small businesses. In many countries the government maintained interest rates arbitrarily low for many years in the face of obviously increasing inflation, and thereby lured many borrowers into housing and other commitments that became oppressive when rates rose materially—especially the steep increases in 1980 and 1981. In all fairness, therefore, governments should cushion the impact of these increased costs on borrowers of limited means.* Revenues from the Investment Levy (and from a TIP, if one is imposed) would help finance this measure, and economic recovery should provide additional government revenues. Unfortunately the opportunity for such help is rapidly receding as time passes, and the damage is becoming irreparable.

Other transitional measures might also be necessary. For example, as the advocates of the MAP point out, an abrupt end to inflation might make it necessary to modify the terms of some agreements that were made before the strategy was implemented and were based on the expectation that inflation would continue.

The External Drain

In the second section of Chapter 7 we observed that balance-of-payments problems would be relatively easy to solve in a world in which all countries maintained high levels of employment at stable prices. However, a single country that found a successful strategy would face a serious drain on its external reserves if its trading partners were still struggling with The Fearsome Dilemma, because measures designed to raise domestic output and employment would also raise the demand for imports. Imported materials and components are incorporated in most

---

* It may be argued that everyone facing increased interest costs for past commitments, including large business firms, should be given relief. The case is much weaker for large firms and for the well-to-do, however. The burden for any borrower is primarily one of short-run cash flows, for persistent inflation implies that the borrower's money income will gradually rise, thereby easing his problem, and that he will eventually recoup his costs as a capital gain. It is those with limited initial resources who suffer, and who may lose their entire investment; the well-to-do will at worst be temporarily inconvenienced. Large firms, by definition, had substantial resources to start with, and any cash-flow problems they meet are likely to reflect normal business risks. Also, they have important tax advantages that permit them to write off their interest costs against other income, and they have probably been able to shift at least a part of the burden to either their customers or their suppliers. Any proposal to give them interest-rate relief raises difficult questions of tax incidence and tax equity.

products nowadays; imported fruits and vegetables supplement domestic output at some seasons or all year; imported consumer goods add variety to consumers' choices; foreign travel offers attractive vacation opportunities; and the demand for all these goods and services rises as income rises. If other countries are not following similarly expansive policies, there will be no corresponding increase in the demand for the first country's exports; its balance of payments will worsen and its external reserves will decline.

In principle, the effects of an import surplus caused by domestic policies to support domestic incomes and employment will spill over into the economies of its trading partners and raise output and employment there, thus stimulating a reciprocal increase in their imports from the first country. Even under the best of circumstances, however, there would be such lags and uncertainties in the process that the first country could not count on it to end the drain before it ran out of reserves, or even to materially reduce it in the foreseeable future. With The Fearsome Dilemma unabated in other countries, the probability is that an increase in their exports would do more to relax their efforts to control inflation than to increase output (since the disciplinary effects of their balance-of-payments positions would be eased), so the reciprocal benefits for the first country would be slight. The others would welcome its initiative, but its external drain would continue.

One possible countermeasure would be to mount an export-promotion program, either as a major engine of domestic expansion or in conjunction with other measures to stimulate output and employment. That would be almost certain to be counterproductive, however, for it would be seen by others as a deliberate effort to export unemployment; they could be counted on to retaliate in one way or another, for example by implementing new protectionist measures of their own, and the net result would be reduced incomes for all. Much the same would apply to protectionist measures in the first country designed to divert spending from imports to domestic goods.

However, it is possible for the first country to implement a set of complementary policies that would allow it to pursue expansionary domestic policies and would prevent an exchange drain yet would leave its uncoöperative trading partners no worse off. The mainstay of the strategy would be to eschew any deliberate encouragement to exports and to rely on measures that would expand domestic output and employment, combined with trade-diverting measures designed to just offset the external drain that would otherwise occur. The trade-diverting measures might take any of several forms—tariffs, quotas, or other devices—which would be protectionist in themselves but defensible as part of a broader strategy. They might well include trade preferences for any other country that chose to follow a similar set of domestic policies. It is true that noncoöperating countries might ignore the expansionist aspect of the policies and attack the protectionist aspect in isolation, but they would do themselves no good by pressing that claim and forcing the first country to abandon its initiative. On the other hand if a strong country with a big domestic market took the initiative it would be in a position to persuade others to join the exercise. In any case countries that chose to coöperate in such a strategy could support one another without giving a free ride to their uncoöperative partners.

Chapter 12
OTHER GOVERNMENT INTERVENTIONS

Promoting a New Social Consensus

All members of the economic community have an interest in maximizing total output, so there will be more real income to be shared. The idea is sometimes put in terms of getting more pie by helping to create a larger pie instead of insisting on a larger slice of a smaller pie. That sounds fine in the abstract, but in practice each participant sees immediate benefits from enlarging his slice, whereas he sees little discernible benefit from anything he can do to enlarge the pie. In principle, the decisions that regulate both the size of the pie and the size of the various slices in a money-and-market economy are made by the impersonal forces of the competitive market. In practice, however, the competitive pricing process degenerates in all too many cases into either a take-it-or-leave-it posture on the part of the seller or a more-or-less-overt confrontation between the representatives of negotiating groups. Perhaps it would be possible to find some way of shifting the emphasis from confrontation to coöperation in the pricing system, just as the various factors of production must coöperate in the productive process.

Sweden has had a long history of industry-wide or nation-wide negotiations between unions and businessmen, with considerable success in resolving the discrepancies between sectoral and national aspirations. The particular combination of circumstances that has made this possible evidently does not exist in other countries, however, and even in Sweden the procedure has encountered difficulties and frictions. Japan has also achieved a social consensus by which it seems able to avoid many of the difficulties experienced in other countries, but it appears to be even more dependent on historical, social, and cultural patterns that would be difficult to reproduce elsewhere. Nevertheless these examples do offer some of the few promising possibilities of getting the public interest recognized in the pricing process.

The time may be ripe for the introduction of nonmonetary incentives and appeals to work for the common good instead of for self-interest. Campaigns of this kind have been used from time to time in various countries, and could doubtless be used again with good effect; pride of work, the simple enjoyment of productive activity, and altruism have surely not disappeared from the earth. The prospect that such incentives could effectively replace the profit motive seems pretty remote, but at the very least they might play a useful supplementary role if they were incorporated in a broader strategy designed to achieve a new social consensus on measures that would not only increase the size of the economic pie but also distribute it in a way that was accepted as fair to all. Such an approach would certainly be compatible with the proposals made in Chapter 11.

Eliminating Waste

Reducing waste in the use of productive resources will not make a direct contribution to resolving The Fearsome Dilemma, because the immediate effects will be like any other reduction of the spending stream: partly a reduction in inflationary pressures and partly a reduction in employment and output. Also, it is necessary to distinguish the essentially-once-for-all effect that correcting a given wasteful procedure will have on the price of the product from the effect of the continuing restraint on pricing decisions that is necessary if inflation is to be eliminated as an on-going process. Indirectly, however, waste-reducing programs should have positive effects for a number of reasons. Some of these effects will stem from psychological factors, in that a careless attitude on the part of the public will encourage price-setters to ask for more, whereas a waste-conscious and price-conscious attitude will encourage them to follow more restrained pricing policies. But the major positive effect should be to focus continuing attention on the more efficient use of productive resources, and thereby to keep costs down.

Some but by no means all the scope for the reduction of wasteful spending in a typical modern economy is to be found in the government sector. Not that all allegations of government waste are to be taken at face value: for example, there is a strong element of self-interest in the criticisms of certain transfer payments (unemployment insurance, welfare assistance, and the like), for the critics are usually in the upper-income groups and would expect to benefit from the tax reductions a decrease in such transfers would make possible. Nevertheless there is no doubt that lax procedures and overly-generous benefits under social legislation can severely weaken work incentives and encourage irresponsibility; there is every reason to eliminate waste and inefficiency in this as in any other field, provided the adequacy of support where needed is not impaired. Also, it is evident that much of the spending under social legislation is absorbed in bureaucratic administrative expenses and does little to help those most in need; many of these programs deserve a thorough re-examination to ensure that the money is spent more effectively.

Waste may result not only from unwise spending by the government or its agencies but also from the methods by which revenue is raised to pay for these activities. The case for paying for most "public goods" out of general revenues is soundly based on the fact that it is either not feasible or not desirable to charge each user for them in the same way that a private enterprise charges its customers for its products. You can't "sell" anyone so many units of national-defence benefits, for example, because he and his family will not consume them exclusively, like the food and clothing they buy; instead, the entire nation shares the benefits no matter who pays for them, so there is no satisfactory way of financing them except out of general tax revenues. In other cases social considerations may dictate that a particular service should be paid for out of general revenues, even though it could be provided on a fee-for-service basis; providing a standard level of education is a good example. Nevertheless there are some public goods that can and should be sold to individual consumers on an essentially-commercial basis like municipal water and sewerage services; where the benefits to the individual can be clearly established and no overriding social considerations are involved, a good case can be made for following normal pricing policies.

To enjoy these goods and services without any specific charge is very convenient, but it may also be wasteful, because there is no way of ensuring that the benefits or the enjoyment derived from them really justify the costs. For example, any one taxpayer pays no more for road maintenance in a given period whether he drives one mile or 1000 miles, or for that matter whether he even owns a car. (Of course he gets other benefits from road maintenance, indirectly, but that does not really alter the argument about how those benefits should be paid for.) We needn't be more specific than that, for road-maintenance or any other service you and I might suggest as a candidate for user-fees might strike others as just the service for which that was **not** appropriate; the point is that wider use of the fee-for-service principle as a means of paying for public goods would probably reduce wasteful use of them.

Similar situations occur in the private sector and in publically-owned utilities. For example, in many jurisdictions telephone subscribers pay a flat monthly fee for local service, whereas a metered charge per call would probably reduce the number and the length of calls and therefore reduce the capital investment required to provide the service. Charges for electricity and other public utilities are sometimes included in the monthly rental of apartments or in the common charges levied on condominium owners, with the result that the individual users have no reason to economize in their use. Waste and inefficiency may occur elsewhere in the private sector too, as noted in the second section of Chapter 5, though it is not easy to prescribe remedies in such cases.

A special case of some practical importance arises with respect to the costs covered by insurance premiums or the equivalent. Automobile insurance, other forms of casualty insurance, and health insurance (or publicly financed health plans) are common examples. The costs of settling a particular claim do not fall directly on the individual who suffers the damage or disability in question, but on his insurance company in the first instance, so consumer resistance to rising costs is greatly weakened. In casualty-insurance cases the policyholder may be tempted to claim more than necessary, since "the insurance company is paying for it"; for example, he may ask for a new fender for his car when the old one could be satisfactorily repaired. In health-insurance cases there may also be some risk of excessive claims or demands for unnecessary service, and doctors may be tempted to prescribe unnecessary procedures; also, strong upward pressure on costs may come from the development of expensive new techniques or equipment aggressively marketed by the producers and too-readily accepted by hospital and health authorities in the name of progress, which the patient will have no reason to oppose. Of course the insurance company will pass all these costs back to the general public in the form of higher insurance premiums, but the individual will see little connection between his own claim and the general increase in premiums.

In all these cases the public's incentive to be economical in its demands on the facilities in question has been inadvertently blunted by modifications of market procedures that have been implemented for reasons that are desirable in themselves, or at least convenient. The wider use of the fee-for-service principle may alleviate the problem when the individual voluntarily chooses to use the product or service, but would not be appropriate for involuntarily incurred costs resulting from misadventures that can be insured against. "Deductibles"—minimum amounts payable by the insured before the insurer becomes liable—help to eliminate small nuisance claims but do not effectively restrain the total claimed. The same is true of experience-rating, i.e. varying the premium according to the past incidence of claims by the particular policyholder. Coinsurance features are sometimes used, such as a provision that the insurer will pay less than 100 percent of the claim, but they do not fully restore consumer resistance to price increases, and they may have unduly-harsh effects on some claimants. It may not be possible to solve all these problems satisfactorily unless innovative new remedies can be devised.

Mergers and Takeovers

An attempt to regulate the purposes for which loans from banks or other financial institutions may be used constitutes an exercise in what is known as "selective" or "qualitative" credit controls, as distinct from the "quantitative" credit controls that central banks endeavour to exercise over banks by the means briefly described in the third section of Chapter 4. Such attempts are usually of limited effectiveness, because a credit-worthy borrower can probably find an alternative source of credit, or else can increase his borrowing for "approved" purposes and thus free up some of his own capital to finance "disapproved" ventures. Nevertheless qualitative credit controls can exert some influence on the uses to which the resources of lending institutions are put; at the very least, they enforce some measure of priority for borrowers whose projects are deemed to be in the public interest. Under inflationary conditions they may be used to discourage mergers or takeovers or speculative ventures that do not appear to serve a useful purpose.

In most countries mergers of business firms or the takeover or acquisition of one firm by another are subject to administrative or judicial review, with the stated aim (not always realized in practice) of protecting the public interest and promoting healthy competition in the marketplace. The problem acquires an additional dimension in an inflationary environment, because speculative considerations become more important.

"Speculation" in the technical sense means engaging in a transaction with the expectation of benefitting from a charge in prices. It can have a desirable and functional effect on prices under appropriate conditions, in that the speculator may perceive an unjustified difference in the market values of certain properties or may perceive a change in the supply conditions for a given commodity, and his intervention may help to rationalize the price structure. An inflationary situation is likely to offer increased opportunities of this kind, because market imperfections and other factors cause some prices to lag behind the general price level and others to move ahead of it. Because of uncertainties of various kinds in product markets and sources of supply, for example, the current prices of equity stocks on formal and informal stock exchanges may not fully reflect the increased replacement cost of the physical assets owned by some companies, perhaps including some major firms. Other firms seeking to expand their productive capacities, or wanting to diversify their activities, may find it is much cheaper to buy out existing firms than to construct new facilities of their own, even if they must pay a substantial premium over the current prices of the target firms' equities.

Mergers and negotiated acquisitions are commonly effected by an exchange of the shares of the new company for those of the old, though sometimes they involve retiring the old shares for cash. Takeovers and aggressive acquisitions, on the other hand, are usually effected by the tender of cash for enough shares to give effective control, or for all shares outstanding, though sometimes by an exchange of shares. In effect, a "friendly" or a negotiated takeover may be indistinguishable from a friendly merger. But takeovers may be predatory rather than friendly, and the target company (or victim) may be forcibly merged with the acquisitor or one of its subsidiaries. An attempted takeover of this kind may be seen as a hostile act by the management of the target company; aggressive tactics may be used on both sides, including all sorts of legal manoeuverings; corporate shareholders or other powerful interests friendly to the target company may make counter-bids; the target company may solicit other takeover offers, in search of a more acceptable partner (a "white knight"); and so on. All of which may add up to a prolonged and expensive fight, from which there may be little if any observable benefit to the general public; on the contrary, there is some presumption that the public interest will suffer from reduced competition in the marketplace.

Not only that, but there is a considerable probability that inflationary pressures will be exacerbated. If the takeover or merger or acquisition is effected by an exchange of shares then the effects on financial markets will likely be small. But if it is financed by borrowing to pay off the original shareholders the story is very different. The effects will be every bit as inflationary as those of borrowing-and-spending for any other purpose. Loan-financed spending for new plant and equipment puts immediate pressure on the available supplies of goods and services, but it also generates a net increase in real wealth and promises greater real output in the future; a loan-financed takeover adds nothing to real wealth or to productive capacity. True, the first effect is merely to inflate stock-market prices but not operating costs, as those bought out try to reinvest the proceeds, but at each round of such asset-chasing there must be some leakage into current spending out of realized capital gains or for other reasons, and in the end this leakage must absorb all the takeover payment except such balances as are permanently retained by investors and added to their pool of funds being held for further ventures.

Even if a takeover is financed out of the liquid resources of the acquisitor itself, the effect will be much the same. Existing portfolio-assets will have to be liquidated, and funds that would otherwise be available to borrowers for normal business purposes will be diverted to buy those assets. Individual takeovers may involve very considerable sums of money, and total takeover activity in a given year may encompass a substantial portion of all the equity stock listed on a nation's stock exchanges.

Much the same results may follow from other speculative actions, such as the purchase and resale of real estate, or the acquisition of any existing asset by investors who see an opportunity for a capital gain.

There is thus a strong case under inflationary conditions for the use of qualitative credit controls to limit the use of borrowed funds for mergers, takeovers, and speculative ventures, particularly with respect to loans from banks and other major financial institutions; exceptions should be made only where the public interest is not endangered, for example to permit family firms to sell out in appropriate circumstances. The typical acquisitor is generally a strong company with a good cash flow or a substantial portfolio of marketable securities, perhaps both, and thus is a very creditworthy applicant for credit from institutional lenders. Takeover financing may therefore crowd normal borrowers out of the market, for purposes that promise little or no public benefit. Qualitative controls under such circumstances may not be 100 percent effective, but they should materially reduce takeover financing and give priority to normal operating loans for productive purposes.

Mortgage Contracts

As noted in the second section of Chapter 9, interest rates are prices and have a legitimate role to play in the decisionmaking process in a money-and-market economy. Attempts to influence or manipulate them may or may not be justified in particular circumstances, but are subject to all the risks and uncertainties of price manipulation generally. Fortunately, the reign of the almost religious belief in low-interest-rates-at-any-cost has been broken by (unfortunately) the inflationary realities of the 1970's and 1980's, and realistic nominal interest rates are again a respectable policy instrument; it is difficult to estimate the economic damage that the prolonged delay in making this adjustment has caused by exacerbating inflationary tendencies, distorting international capital flows, and other disturbances to the decisionmaking process.

Nevertheless inflation brings increases in nominal interest rates that may have effects on innocent bystanders serious enough to justify some intervention. One of the transitional measures suggested in Chapter 11 was the provision of interest-rate relief in certain cases. More permanent measures may also be necessary, at least until inflation is clearly overcome, in the expectation that realistic monetary policies will cause interest rates to fluctuate over a considerable range in the future. Some new types of mortgage-loan contracts are being tested in some jurisdictions to help homeowners, and similar techniques might be considered for small businesses, farmers, fishermen, and perhaps other groups deemed worthy of assistance in confronting the problems that interest-rate fluctuations bring. Some lenders, for example, are offering lower interest rates on contracts that give the lender a share in any capital appreciation of the property on resale or at the end of an agreed period. Such contracts reduce the immediate cost of the loan to the homeowner, but at the sacrifice of a portion of the equity in his home.

Mortgage lenders in some countries have long followed the practice of allowing the interest rate to vary during the term of the loan and setting the monthly combined payment of interest and capital at a fixed sum, related to family income and other considerations. This alleviates the impact of unexpected increases in interest rates on the family budget, though it means that the capital-repayment portion decreases and the repayment period is stretched out farther and farther into the future. Another technique now being explored in some areas is to set the monthly payment at less than the interest charges alone when nominal interest rates are high, and to raise the monthly payments gradually over the term of the contract; in effect a part of the interest costs in the early years is capitalized. These two techniques could be combined in one contract, which would permit both variations in the interest rate on some agreed basis and the capitalization of some of the interest charges in the early years. Provision would have to be made for escalating the monthly payments as the mortgagor's income rose, and it would probably be necessary to offer the lender some form of insurance against default, since the loan might well come to exceed the value of the property for a time. There would also have to be some means of protecting the homeowner from getting into too expensive a contract, i.e. from getting carried away and taking on a more expensive house than a realistic view of his future prospects would warrant.

Government Spending Initiatives

Typical government sectors nowadays are major purchasers of goods and services, and account for a substantial percentage of total spending in the economy. At the very least, careful attention to their buying policies should offer important opportunities to promote competitive pricing and to inform the public of price and quality comparisons. Given proper authority, government purchasing agents could take an even more hard-nosed approach to keeping prices down: on the basis of an agreed volume purchased for government use, they might negotiate a reduction in the prices to be charged the general public for the same goods and services.

Even at the best of times some individuals are bound to experience temporary unemployment, for seasonal reasons or because of market changes that require the shift of resources from one industry to another, and suitable cushioning devices will ensure that the burden is shared equitably: unemployment-insurance benefits that are reasonably close to the individual's normal wage or salary, benefit periods that are automatically extended if the unemployment rate rises materially, and that sort of thing. Special measures are necessary for young people just entering the labour force, not only because they will not have had an opportunity to build up an employment record sufficient to give them eligibility for unemployment-insurance benefits of material value if they do find work and are then laid off, but also because it is important for them to develop good work habits at this critical stage of their working lives: delay in landing their first permanent job may have serious psychological effects on them and may lead to anti-social attitudes. Universally-portable pension and other benefits and other aids to labour mobility are also desirable.

These cushioning devices are doubly useful when inflation gets out of hand or threatens to do so. Temporary fiscal and monetary restraints have a legitimate role to play in such circumstances, while more permanent remedies are sought. In that context the unemployment and lost output these measures will bring are unfortunate short-term side effects of the corrective policies, **not** (as some would have it) an intentional technique for disicipling excessive wage demands. Adequate cushioning devices permit the restraining policies to be pursued more vigourously and to be more quickly effective. Presumably these devices should be financed by increased taxes, since this scenario implies that increased government deficits would be inappropriate in the circumstances.

It can be argued that the government should introduce a permanent policy of providing employment at all times to anyone unable to find a better alternative, despite the bad reputation earned by Works Progress Administration (W.P.A.) projects in the U.S.A. and similar make-work projects elsewhere in the 1930's. The one really effective full-employment policy is a job opportunity for everyone who wants it; it would be a cushioning device *par excellence*. A hundred years ago Victor Hugo, in one of the many discursive passages in *Les Misérables*, flatly asserted that "work can not be a rule without being a right"—if work is the way to earn food and survival, then work is a right.[1] In those days, of course, governments took no responsibility for the overall performance of the economy, and unemployment was the scourge of the ordinary citizen, who at best lived all too close to the lower limit of survival. Today's governments have gone a long way towards accepting this responsibility through commitments to high-employment policies, but these policies are now undermined (temporarily, we hope) by inflationary pressures, and at best they fall short of Hugo's proposition that work is a matter of right.

Perhaps some form of guaranteed employment opportunities could be implemented, designed to combine training and retraining programs with the pursuit of meaningful and constructive activities, including special programs for new entrants to the labour force. They might offer a remuneration of not less than some standard percentage of his last wage or salary to anyone laid off for any cause other than unsatisfactory performance, and remuneration on a scale related to skills and training for others. Every effort should be made to employ these people on tasks worthy of their abilities or in training programs appropriate to their capabilities; surely we **have** learned **something** in this field since the 1930's! The cost of such a program should not be excessive, considering the magnitude of the benefits that might result and considering that, in the absence of such a program, substantially similar costs will be incurred for sterile dead-end forms of public assistance to the indigent.

A Cost-Based Tax Policy

Tax-based incomes policies (TIP's) were briefly described in the fourth section of Chapter 10. It is possible that the wage restraints decided on in pursuance of the suggestions in Chapter 11 might take the form of some version of a TIP, for that offers several attractions. Labour leaders might favour it because it would permit them to negotiate meaningfully with each individual employer, without being rigidly bound by a global formula, and thus they could deal more effectively with local issues. Employers might like it for the same reason, i.e. that it would give the individual firm more flexibility in negotiations, and because it would retain the discipline of normal market forces in large degree.

However, TIP's have another interesting feature from the community's point of view: they make use of a tax addressed to business **costs** rather than income or profits. (This is also a characteristic of the Market Anti-Inflation Plan, which is likewise described in Chapter 10.) Regardless of whether some form of TIP is ever implemented, the idea of a cost-based tax policy is worth exploring, for it would give the firm a double incentive to reduce costs, as noted at the end of Chapter 10.

There are several possibilities. One approach would be to impose a surcharge on the corporation tax, and to marry it with the target-price technique used in some wartime contracts.* This would involve a minimum departure from present tax measures. For each of his major products a producer might be subjected to progressively higher surcharges for increases in average costs in one year over the previous year, and given progressively greater tax rebates for decreases. There would be problems with such things as ensuring that quality was maintained (or rewarding improvements in quality), the introduction of new products, measuring the volume of intangible services, etc., just as there would be with the TIP or the MAP, but it should be possible to work out procedures that would apply to a large portion of total real output. As with some TIP proposals, direct compliance might be limited (initially at least) to a relatively few large firms, and extended more generally if experience indicated that that would be desirable. The target-cost aspect should discourage firms from simply factoring the tax into their cost structures, especially if the penalty for exceeding the target was made sufficiently high at the margin.

If it proved impractical to set meaningful annual target prices for a sufficient portion of total real output, more comprehensive if somewhat cruder methods might be used. Two variants suggest themselves. One would be a tax applied to any increase in a firm's total costs in the year, or a tax credit for a decrease; the tax rate would have to be high enough to ensure that higher costs precluded higher profits, but the increase in costs would have to be measured relative to some suitable index of the firm's total real output. A second variant would be a flat tax on all costs each year; the rate should be high enough to impose a material but not a confiscatory burden on typical net profits. This variant would be cruder than the first, but simpler to apply.

A more radical version would be to replace the corporation tax altogether by a tax on all business costs. The tax base would include wages and all other forms of personal remuneration, the cost of all materials and services purchased, interest, capital-cost allowances, and any other imputed costs except the write-off of losses. This tax should be integrated with the personal income-tax along the lines indicated in the following section.

Regardless of whether business taxes are levied on costs or on net income, the authorities might offer special incentives for reducing any

---

* To get away from the disincentives to economy inherent in cost-plus contracts when it was impracticable to make reliable estimates of the cost of untried products, some contracts set target prices and offered graduated bonuses for below-target costs and graduated penalties for above-target costs.

cost components that are considered particularly nonproductive from the community's point of view. Many observers would nominate advertising and other selling costs for such attention, despite the caveats noted in the last section of Chapter 6, though other candidates could undoubtedly be found as well. These expenditures form a substantial part of total business costs. They certainly do perform a useful function in informing the general public about what products and services are available and in encouraging comparative shopping, but beyond some rather imprecise point they become merely defensive and mutually-offsetting outlays. Under a cost-based tax system these or other unproductive costs in excess of a stipulated limit could be assessed at (say) double or triple their actual amount. Under an income-based system they could be made ineligible for inclusion in deductible expenses when computing taxable income.

Tax Equity

We argued in Chapter 8 that the progressivity of the tax system in many jurisdictions has been badly eroded in recent years, and in Chapter 9 we asserted that the main criticism of current government deficits is that they benefit the wrong people. The clear implication is that remedial measures are in order.

One of the buzz-words in public-finance circles these days is "tax-expenditures." The term sounds confusing, but the idea behind it is simple enough. Most tax measures (especially income-tax measures) exempt certain otherwise-taxable items, so the government forgoes a portion of the potential revenue at the source; the effect is the same as if the revenue was first collected and then paid out again as a transfer payment to the taxpayer, hence the name. However, these transfer payments are a special kind of expenditure, in that they do not appear in the government's accounts and do not have to be passed anew each year as normal budgetary expenditures do. Once incorporated in the law, an exemption or tax-expenditure escapes further legislative attention indefinitely. Most tax shelters are in this category.

One example is the use-value or rental-value of an owner-occupied house. In many jurisdictions this is not taxed as income, or is not taxed at its full worth. Suppose two people with the same number of dependents, identical salaries, and identical wealth live side by side in identical houses worth $100,000; one has invested his capital in his house and owns it outright, and pays $3,000 for insurance and municipal taxes on it, while the other rents his house for $12,000 a year and holds a $100,000 security portfolio that yields him $9,000 annually. Each receives a net benefit of $9,000 from his investment, but the second must declare his as interest-income and pay tax on it, whereas the first is not taxed on his essentially-similar benefit (technically known as an "imputed rent"). Different tax treatment of people in essentially-similar circumstances is recognized as inequitable, so a good case can be made for taxing the homeowner on the imputed rent he receives on his equity. Furthermore, it is the well-to-do who are in the best position to use this tax shelter.

Now suppose inflation sets in. The nominal value of each house rises; the renter's rent rises with inflation, only partly offset by an increase in his nominal interest-income (after tax) from his investment; the homeowner's tax-free imputed rental income increases proportionately. Thus the homeowner gets a double windfall—the capital value of his house rises, and his advantage in after-tax income increases. The case for taxing him on his imputed rental income is strengthened, and his windfall gains make it a good time to impose the tax.

Many other shelters for investment income are provided in the complex array of tax-exemptions and tax-expenditures to be found in most national tax systems. Some are completely unexceptionable in themselves, or are even laudable, aside from the fact that they escape the annual review they would get if they were incorporated in the normal budgetary process. Nevertheless, skillful use of the available shelters permits some wealthy individuals to avoid paying any income-tax at all. However, they are too numerous and they vary too much from country to country to permit full treatment here. It will suffice to raise one other question of tax equity, namely the corporation tax, because it is a major one in its own right and because many tax-expenditures are addressed to corporations.

It is a common practice nowadays in most jurisdictions to tax corporations as if they were persons, but under a different rate schedule. Since all corporations are ultimately owned by natural persons, economists have long argued that their incomes should not be taxed separately but as the incomes of their ultimate owners. Sometimes the argument is based on the fact that the corporate income may otherwise be taxed twice—once in the hands of the corporation and then as dividends in the hands of the shareholder. However, the net effect of double taxation is merely to raise the effective tax rate; whether that is fair or not depends on the total tax levied on the income and how it compares with the tax levied on the same amount of income derived from other sources. Some taxpayers may indeed pay disproportionately-large taxes for this reason, but for the most part that just means they failed to seek good tax-planning advice. The fact is that corporations benefit from such a wide range of tax-exemptions and tax-expenditures that the taxes they actually pay in a typical case may be far below the standard rates nominally applied to them, and wealthy investors have additional tax havens for their personal incomes. Far from causing excessive inroads by the tax collector, in many cases the corporation tax allows the ultimate owners to reinvest a substantial portion of their incomes as retained corporate earnings and pay relatively low taxes thereon.

There is a vast literature on the subject of corporate taxation and whether personal and corporate income-taxes should be integrated. For our purposes it will be enough to offer two comments. First, integration would certainly involve many problems and complexities, as its critics claim. Second, that does not detract from the argument that the possibility of integration should be carefully considered; the proposal is not to attempt the impossible task of devising a tax system that is free of all faults, but merely to maintain a continuing effort to make national tax systems more equitable.

Interest as a Business Cost

An outstanding example of inadvertent damage to the price-cost structure is the rather arbitrary administrative practice, followed almost universally, of treating interest payments by business enterprises as deductible costs for income-tax purposes, instead of as simply one form of factor returns to capital. This copies standard accounting practice and is entirely logical from that point of view, which is addressed primarily to the interests of the owner. It is quite illogical as a basis for levying taxes, and introduces distortions that are intensified in inflationary times.

Business enterprises finance their capital requirements either by offering shares (the issue of equity capital) or by borrowing (the issue of debt capital). From the point of view of the economist, these are simply alternative forms of financial capital, which differ primarily in the terms on which they are supplied: the latter has a prior claim to an agreed rate of return and to the repayment of the principal at maturity, the former is the residual claimant on earnings and assets, and is repayable only out of the proceeds of winding up the enterprise. Returns to debt capital are in the form of interest, returns to equity capital are in the form of some combination of dividends paid out and income retained within the enterprise. Yet these essentially-similar factor returns are commonly treated very differently for business-tax purposes; debt returns escape tax at this stage, and the levy falls solely on equity returns.

From the point of view of the business enterprise, debt and equity are partly alternative and partly complementary sources of capital. They are alternative because needed capital can be raised by either or by some combination of the two. They are complementary because investors are unlikely to provide debt capital unless normal business risks are adequately covered by a cushion of equity capital, and a prudently limited debt structure may finance additional productive capacity and thus add to the net earnings on equity. The distinction is most meaningful for an enterprise in which the equity is closely held by a cohesive group. Confusion arises in the case of corporate enterprises because of the legal fiction that they are "persons"; it is compounded when corporate equity is widely held. The individual shareholder may have little more control over the corporation than the creditor, despite the fact that in concert with other shareholders he retains (and on occasion may exercise) the legal right to discharge the management team and replace it with another. This situation is further complicated by the fact that a corporation's equity stock may be subdivided into a number of classes with very different rights to dividends and very different claims on retained profits or assets, some of which classes are more akin to debt issues than to common equity issues.

From the point of view of the investor, the choice between buying debt contracts and buying equity contracts is primarily a matter of comparative returns: a relatively assured return in the one case, possibly greater but less-sure returns in the other. He may buy new issues of both categories indifferently if he judges their prospects attractive, and may trade them actively on secondary markets according to his changing assessment of current and future conditions, strongly influenced by expectations of capital gains or losses as well as interest and dividends.

Thus the distinction between the two categories becomes blurred for both the corporation and the investing public. Corporate capital structures may include a variety of security issues that constitute a virtually-continuous spectrum from pure debt through debt issues that are conditionally or unconditionally convertible into some form of equity, preferred shares that may or may not closely resemble debt contracts, and nonvoting or otherwise-restricted ordinary or common shares, to the purest of equities. The current returns to issues on one side of a legally determinate but economically uninteresting point on the spectrum are deemed to be interest and are deducted as a business cost by the issuer, those on the other side are deemed to be dividends or retained earnings and must come out of after-tax profits.

For the most part the issues raised by the unequal treatment of these two essentially similar returns to capital lie in the field of public finance and taxation, and are beyond the scope of this book. However, it contributes to the price-cost distortions of inflation, and inflation exacerbates some of its distorting effects on economic decisionmaking. It biases business capitalization towards a top-heavy debt structure, which makes an enterprise vulnerable in slack times or when interest rates rise sharply. Also, it means that the borrowing costs of established business enterprises are shared (subsidized) by the governments to which the taxes are payable.

Other borrowers get no such subsidy, notwithstanding that many of them are surely more deserving of special consideration in getting access to capital. Regional and local governments borrowing for community purposes such as water and sewage plants, roads, and other public works get no tax subsidy, nor do non-profit enterprises, nor developing countries attempting to provide infrastructure and other desperately needed capital facilities for which they must seek funds in world capital markets. New business enterprises have little or no taxable income in their formative years when they are most vulnerable to adverse events, whether they are domiciled in the developed countries or struggling to become established in the developing countries. All these borrowers must compete for funds on unequal terms with established business borrowers, who are in effect able to lay off forty or fifty percent of their net borrowing costs on the tax collector. Inflation greatly worsens the problem, because it usually brings a sharp increase in nominal interest rates and therefore in the relative interest costs of disadvantaged borrowers.

Another little-noticed effect of the favourable treatment of interest costs for business-tax purposes is that it greatly weakens the efficacy of monetary policy in restraining inflation. In principle, high interest rates should choke off marginally profitable capital outlays and thereby reduce the spending stream. But the tax-subsidy to business interest costs for established firms reduces that disciplinary effect and puts the main burden on other borrowers who get no such help. And, since tax-sheltered business borrowing is a large part of the total borrowing in the economy, monetary restraint must be much greater than it would otherwise need to be in order to have the desired effect. Which means, of course, that interest costs for other borrowers must also be correspondingly higher.

There is thus a strong case for ceasing to allow the deduction of interest payments as a business expense and treating them on a par with dividends and retained earnings as simply a somewhat different form of return to those who put up the capital with which a business operates. That would greatly improve the effectiveness of monetary policy, especially in an inflationary environment, because it would place the whole cost of business borrowing where it belongs. It would probably reduce business demands for borrowed funds and cause a shift of capital structures to increased reliance on equity claims, thus tending to reduce interest rates and to make more debt financing available to other borrowers. Even if it had no net effect on interest rates or on the availability of funds, however, it would improve the relative position of nonbusiness borrowers.

There would of course be certain difficulties to overcome, but most of them could be met by an effective integration of the corporate and the personal income taxes, which most economists advocate in any case. Briefly, a business enterprise would compute the net excess of income over expenditure before considering either interest or dividend payments (i.e. all out-of-pocket costs for labour and materials, plus capital-cost allowances and similar charges). If the corporation tax continued to be levied against profits rather than costs it would be applied to the excess just described and treated as a withholding tax on returns to the suppliers of capital. If the tax were levied against costs instead of profits, then the withholding tax would be applied to **total** costs, including actual or imputed returns to invested capital, in order to ensure that the cost-cutting incentive applied to all factor inputs. (There are several ways in which this could be done, which we need not go into here; perhaps the simplest would be to apply the tax to the sum of labour and material costs, capital-cost allowances, and an imputed rate of return on the depreciated value of the business's assets as derived from the application of the depreciation rates allowed for tax purposes).

The withholding tax would resemble that now deducted from wages and salaries in many tax jurisdictions, and would be set at some standard rate by the taxing authorities. Deductions at this standard rate would be made during the year from the interest payments made to creditors, so the enterprise would not be out of pocket for this portion of the tax levied against it, but no such deduction would need to be made from dividends because they would come from the tax-paid funds remaining in the hands of the firm, hence it would be immaterial whether the funds accruing to the shareholders were paid out in dividends or retained within the firm. Individual tax-payers would report their interest receipts and their *pro rata* share of other business income on a gross basis (i.e. before deducting the withholding tax), but would receive credit for the withholding tax against their overall income-tax liability. A new structure of income-tax rates would be compiled, presumably designed to give about the same total yield as previously obtained from personal and corporate taxes combined. Provision would have to be made for avoiding double-counting of income received by one business enterprise from another and then paid out to its own creditors in turn—especially banks and other financial institutions which act as intermediaries between primary lenders (their depositors) and ultimate borrowers.

Chapter 13
THE INTERNATIONAL FIELD

The Key-Currency Problem Revisited

There are three changes in current practices in the international mone-tary sphere that would certainly reduce imported inflation, and there is an important danger to be avoided in current proposals to liberalize the conditions under which international aid is available to countries with balance-of-payments deficits. The three changes are the reform or abolition of the key-currency system, new procedures for issuing Special Drawing Rights to Fund members, and improved surveillance of lending by one central bank to another. The danger to be avoided is the undue relaxation of the terms on which Fund members have access to its resources. All four of these current practices or proposals are condoned if not actually advocated by economic policymakers in leading chancel-leries of the world, who should know better, in apparent disregard for their inflationary implications.

Surely the most obviously needed change in current international practices is to put an end to the acceptance without limit of the domestic monies of certain nations as international monies. This is the essence of what Robert Triffin has been advocating in many articles and books since soon after the end of World War II.[1] The evil consequences have been explained in the fifth section of Chapter 4: the automatic monetiza-tion of the balance-of-payments deficits of key-currency countries. It is the international equivalent of what used to happen at the national level when a government issued its own currency notes: the amount and timing of the issues were usually directly related to the appetite of the government for "cheap" financing, not to the needs of the economy for a money supply appropriate to the current level of real output. It proved very expensive instead of cheap, because the expansion of the currency not only was inflationary in itself but also brought a secondary expan-sion of money and money-substitutes through the banking system. It gradually came to be recognized that the public interest was better served by putting the currency issue in charge of some body that was indepen-dent of the government—usually a privately-owned bank of issue, the precursor of the modern money-managing central bank.

Remedies and Alternatives

It can be argued that the ideal solution would be an international agreement to establish what may be called a supracentral bank under strong management, whose obligations would be the only universally-acceptable international money and the only form in which any nation's external reserves could be held. It would be a central bank of central banks, i.e. it would stand in relation to national central banks in just the same way they stand in relation to the commercial banks operating in their jurisdictions, and would provide an elastic but carefully-regulated supply of international money to the world. The extent to which and the terms on which present forms of reserves—meaning the gold, key-currency balances, and claims on the International Monetary Fund now held by national monetary authorities—would be converted into the new reserve asset would have to be determined by international negotiation, and need not concern us here: the essential point is that the use of the **national** currency of any particular country as an **international** money would be terminated, and new accruals of key currencies would no longer be recognized as part of the official reserves of the receiving country. Any country and its residents would remain free to accept and hold whatever balances in whatever currencies they chose, subject only to such general limitations as the international community might find necessary to ensure that no national currency became a substitute on a significant scale for the new reserve medium (i.e. that it did not become an important reserve medium *de facto* instead of *de jure*).

Not everyone would agree that a supracentral bank issuing a new universal reserve medium is the ideal solution to the key-currency problem. For example, those who believe all exchange rates should be allowed to fluctuate freely would probably see it as biased towards a fixed-rate system and would therefore object to it on principle. However, we can easily steer a safe passage between the Scylla of a supracentral bank and the Charybdis of the fixed-versus-fluctuating-exchange-rate debate. We avoid the first by noting that the essential point is merely to find some effective way of regulating the quantity of international money available at any particular time, or the increase permitted during a given period. We avoid the second by noting that fluctuating exchange-rates will not in themselves solve key-currency balance-of-payments deficits, because they do not prevent residents of the key-currency country from paying for imported goods by tendering their own local currency to the foreign exporter. So doing will indeed tend to depreciate the exchange value of that currency and thus deter external purchases, but the feedback effects noted in Chapter 4 will tend to raise domestic prices and maintain the competitiveness of imports.

At first sight you might think it would be easy enough to end the key-currency role of any national money: the monetary authorities and the residents of other countries should just refuse to accept it in payment for goods and services. In practice, however, it is not so easy. Even though its purchasing power is seen to be steadily dropping, any one individual need not hesitate to accept it because he can be pretty sure he can pass it on to someone else, like a hot potato, before it depreciates materially in his hands. That, after all, is why any form of money is accepted, whether it be a domestic currency or some other, and whether its purchasing power is depreciating or not. Besides, his choice is basically between accepting the key currency or forgoing the sale altogether—and he may well be able to exact a higher price when selling for a depreciated currency.

The monetary authorities of the exporter's country may be in no better position to refuse to accept key currencies. If they are trying to stabilize the exchange rate of their currency relative to a key currency, or even just trying to keep the rate floating within reasonable bounds, they may have to add more to their holdings of the key currency than they really want. Major nations, regardless of their exchange-rate policies, may find themselves constrained to accumulate surplus balances of the key currency or else permit the foreign-exchange market to become badly disorganized. In any case too adamant a refusal to accept any additions to their key-currency balances may mean that their exporters are priced out of foreign markets or in other ways are forced to forgo sales they might otherwise make—a particularly difficult choice if unemployment is a problem in the domestic economy, as it is in most countries today.

The ultimate solution, of course, is for the key-currency country to end its deficits. But to expect this to be done overnight is like telling a drowning man all he has to do is stop drowning. A chronic deficit in any country's balance of payments means that its domestic output is not sufficiently competitive and hence its exports are not paying for its imports;* it can only be corrected by either attracting previously-unemployed resources into the production of goods and services that are competitive with the products of other countries on domestic and foreign markets, or diverting spending from imports to domestically produced goods and services at competitive prices. Furthermore, the second alternative is only viable in a world that is enjoying approximately full employment and in which resources can be shifted from one

---

* This tacitly assumes that the net flow of domestic saving is just sufficient to pay for net new investment in productive capital goods. To be more precise, a balance-of-payments deficit for a country that is borrowing abroad to finance some of its domestic capital expenditure means that its exports plus its net borrowings do not pay for all its imports; for a capital-exporting country, it means that its exports do not cover its imports plus its net lending abroad.

occupation to another fairly easily, otherwise it will be seen to be an attempt to "export unemployment" and will invite retaliation. An example of what is required has been advocated in the U.S.A. as "the reindustrialization of America": the revitalizing of the economy by a new social contract, including a new sense of teamwork among all economic sectors and social groups.[2] It **can** be done—for proof you have only to look at the reindustrialization of Europe and Japan after World War II—but it will not be easy and it will take a long time.

Nevertheless there are ways of ending the automatic monetization of continuing key-currency balance-of-payments deficits, if a sufficient degree of international coöperation can be mustered. A major consideration will be to find a form of agreement that does not require the acquiescence of the key-currency countries themselves—which in practice means that it must be outside the councils of the International Monetary Fund, where the key-currency countries presently hold an effective veto. You can not expect them to be enthusiastic about giving up their ability to foist their balance-of-payments problems onto others willy-nilly. Looking at the U.S.A. in particular, the idea that it should show an attitude of "benign neglect" in this field, i.e. should let others worry about its deficit, is not as vocally advocated now as it once was, but it has not yet been really scotched either.

There is no denying that U.S. balance-of-payments deficits must be financed somehow over a reasonable adjustment period; any attempt to force an end to them forthwith would be not only unduly harsh on the U.S. economy but also extremely disruptive of world trade in general. The point is merely that they must not be financed by automatic additions to the world supply of international money; they must be financed in essentially the same way and subject to essentially the same discipline as the deficits of other countries, i.e. by persuading others to lend the money at commercial rates of interest, within prudent expectations of repayment over an acceptable period of time. No one country could insist on such terms for its trade with the U.S.A., because that would merely drive a large part of its export sales to competitors in other countries. However, a group of nations comprising the major creditors of the U.S.A. could do so by acting in concert, and would probably have enough bargaining power to elicit the effective coöperation of the U.S. authorities. Indeed, an enlightened U.S. administration might well take the lead in negotiating such an agreement.

At the same time we must be wary of "solutions" that merely mask the automatic monetization of key-currency deficits instead of financing them in more acceptable ways. Suppose, for example, that something resembling what we have called a supracentral bank is established. In that case an immediate decision will have to be made as to how the central banks of member nations will get their initial allocations of the new reserve medium, and how they can acquire additional amounts of this new international money in the future. The obvious answer to the first question is that each nation's central bank will turn over some or all of its existing reserves (gold, Fund positions, and key-currency balances) to the new institution in exchange for an equivalent amount of the new money. As for the second question, suppose that every nation's central bank is allowed to exchange any additional key-currency balances it may acquire from time to time, without limit. That would simply perpetuate the monetization of key-currency balance-of-payments deficits in a much more dangerous form—more dangerous because the deficit would now be financed not just by the key-currency country's IOU's but by an internationally-backed universal reserve asset. It would be like allowing a nation's commercial banks to determine for themselves how much reserves the central bank should allow them.

Or as if a national government had turned the management of its currency over to an insufficiently-independent bank of issue, and then forced the bank to lend it whatever amount it demanded—i.e., proceeded to stuff its central bank with government paper. That would provide the nation's commercial banks with excess reserves on a grand scale, and lead to a multiple credit expansion. It would be just a slightly more sophisticated means of giving the government access to apparently cheap but really expensive financing by issuing its own currency notes. And don't say that that idea is so ridiculous that it would never get a hearing from any reputable international body! Some versions of the proposed "substitution account" that surfaces from time to time would apparently amount to just such a procedure: accruals of unwanted U.S.-dollar balances could be "voluntarily" paid in to the substitution account in exchange for I.M.F. obligations that would be universally accepted as international reserve assets.

Special Drawing Rights

That brings us to the second change in procedures in the international monetary field that would reduce the infectious spread of imported inflation: the way Special Drawing Rights (SDR's) are allocated and distributed among members of the Fund. Briefly, the SDR is an unconditional right of a member to draw on the Fund's resources to meet a balance-of-payments deficit. The hope is that it will eventually become the only (or at least the major) external-reserve asset and international money, replacing gold and key currencies: hence the popular sobriquet "paper gold". That would enable the international community to "manage" the supply of international reserves available to the world in pretty much the same way that national central banks manage the reserves available to domestic commercial banks. The first allotment was decided on in 1969, and amounted to 9.3-billion SDR's (at that time the SDR was valued at US$1.00) in three annual instalments. A second allocation of about 12-billion SDR's was agreed to in 1978, again divided into three annual installments, and a third allocation has now been proposed. (The value of the SDR has varied from US$1.00 to about US$1.35; at the end of 1983 it was about US$1.10.) These decisions are taken by the Executive Board of the I.M.F., composed of representatives appointed or elected by individual members or groups of members.

If this is viewed as a form of supracentral banking managed by an international committee, it has had a most inauspicious start. The first allocation of SDR's was made on the basis of estimates that the "need" for reserves would grow at a rate of between 4-billion and 5-billion SDR's per annum over the next three years, and that the supply from sources other than SDR's would grow by between 1-billion and 1.5-billion SDR's per annum. The estimate of the need for reserves seemed a bit high, for it implied an average compound growth rate of 5 to 6 percent per annum, double that of the two preceding decades, whereas some economists thought that the existing level of reserves was already too high. Perhaps there was some confusion in some people's minds between the need for reserves-to-hold, i.e. true reserves against contingencies, and reserves-to-spend, i.e. access to external sources of capital. But, whatever may be said in defence of the estimate of the need for reserves, the Fund's estimate of the growth of reserves in other forms than SDR's proved grossly inadequate. For starters, it assumed that the balance-of-payments deficits of the key-currency countries (Britain and the U.S.A.) would soon be brought under control. Of course no such thing happened, and in fact "other" forms of reserves grew by 59-billion SDR's in those three years, not 3-billion to 4.5-billion—an increase of 76 percent instead of 4 to 6 percent. (See the table on page 40.) Nevertheless, incredible as it may seem, the Fund allowed the second and third installments of the first SDR allocation to proceed on schedule.

Parenthetically, it may be noted that it was widely believed at that time (and probably still is) that key-currency balance-of-payments deficits are necessary to provide the rest of the world with increases in reserves. Nothing could be further from the truth. Key-currency deficits do indeed add equivalently to the international reserves held by others (for the most part in "undigested" and therefore inflation-inducing form), but any reasonably-well-managed country can normally add to its reserves-to-hold (true or "digested" reserves) even if the key-currency countries are enjoying **surpluses** in their balances of payments. That is what major capital markets are all about: supplying the legitimate needs of credit-worthy borrowers, whether domestic or foreign and whether in the private or the public sector. If a country wants to add to its reserves it ought to be able to do so by factoring that objective into its external borrowing program; the net cost will normally be small, i.e. the difference between the interest paid on an equal amount of external debt and the interest earned on the investment of its reserves.*

No allocations of SDR's were made between 1973 and 1977, yet global reserves rose another 79 percent. But in 1978 the Fund decided that a new allocation was in order. This time the decision was attributed mainly to promoting the SDR's as the primary reserve asset of the international monetary system, and procedural changes were made to increase its usefulness. This, despite the fact that the seventh general increase in Fund quotas (and therefore in the resources available to it) was pending, and despite the fact that this time no-one was predicting an early end to the monetization of key-currency deficits. However, about a quarter of the new subscriptions was made payable in SDR's, thus diverting about 5-billion SDR's of the new allocations into the general resources of the Fund.

Again these decisions and actions may be put in perspective by visualizing corresponding events in the domestic affairs of a particular country. Would any central banker in his right mind commit himself to the expansion of commercial-bank reserves on a rigid schedule over the following three years regardless of what happened in the economy? Would he base his decision about the amount of the expansion on a mere pious hope that the supply of alternative reserve assets for the commercial banks would somehow be curtailed? Would he proceed with the planned expansion when it became clear that alternative forms of bank reserves were growing explosively? Would he start a new expansion on a similarly rigid schedule nine years later, while the growth of alternative forms of reserves showed no signs of slackening? Would he justify this action as a way of enhancing his influence on the domestic financial

---

*Of course, a prudent administration must weigh the net costs against the net advantages of maintaining contingency reserves. There may be times when even the most prudent nation may have difficulty in financing even the most promising of development programs, in which case it may quite properly reassess the risk and reduce its contingency reserves below what it would like in order to finance priority projects. In a rationally operating world, however, the response of capital-exporting nations would be to ensure an adequate supply of development capital to such countries, not to encourage key-currency countries to mismanage their economies as a means of financing third-country development projects.

system? Well, that is what supracentral banking by an international committee has done. Surely it is time for a new deal.

Inter-Central-Bank Borrowing

There is still a third change in present practices that would reduce the spread of imported inflation: more effective international surveillance of lending by one central bank to another.

If the central bank of a key-currency country lends to the central bank of another country, it is clear that new international reserves are "created": the lending bank writes up a deposit on the liabilities side of its balance sheet in favor of the borrowing bank, which the latter is then free to use for reserve purposes, and writes up a loan receivable on the assets side. Though it is less obvious, the effect is essentially the same if the central bank of a non-key-currency country makes a loan to another central bank. In this case the loan is effectively made out of the lending bank's holdings of a key currency, but it will treat its loan receivable as an asset denominated in the key currency and therefore to all intents and purposes a reserve asset which it will fully expect to reclaim if its balance of payments turns adverse. Or, alternatively, you may prefer to say that otherwise-idle key-currency balances (external reserves) have been activated, i.e. put into general circulation in international payments, which comes to about the same thing as far as the borrower and third countries are concerned. Inter-bank borrowings of this kind do not usually account for a large part of total international reserves, but their volume may become substantial in times of crisis, or when the supply of reserves from other sources is deemed inadequate. For the effective management of global reserves, therefore, they should be explicitly taken into account.

Access to Fund Drawings

Access to the general resources of the International Monetary Fund actually involves getting the currencies of (or claims against) the central banks of other member countries, and so may be said to come within the compass of inter-central-bank borrowing:* technically speaking the Fund merely sells its holdings of the borrower's currency (not necessarily a key currency) in exchange for increased holdings of the borrower's

---

* The same was originally true of the use of the SDR, but in this case the Fund merely acted as referee to ensure fairness among members in selecting the "currencies convertible in fact" to be exchanged for SDR's. Since 1978 the SDR has been freely transferable between members.

currency. However, there are two important differences. First, the right to draw from the Fund within prescribed limits is included in a member's external reserves as officially compiled, so drawings constitute the activation of previously-idle reserves rather than the creation of new reserves, though as already noted the net effect is essentially the same. Second, the borrower's obligation is to repay the Fund, not necessarily in the same currency as the drawing, whereas the country whose currency is drawn gets an equivalent increase in its claims against the general resources of the Fund: the increase in international reserves thus takes the form of a claim with a degree of "moneyness" that is more universal than and hence superior to a claim against the central bank of any one country. It is therefore clear that access to the Fund's resources must be prudently managed in order to minimize the risk that inflationary excesses will be encouraged in the world economy.

You will note that we said to **minimize** the risk of inflationary excesses, not to **eliminate** it. You could say that the very essence of the Fund's operations is to strike a proper balance between the need for the discipline imposed on the domestic policies of member countries by balance-of-payments considerations, and the need to cushion that discipline against the unnecessarily-disruptive shocks that may result from a wide variety of economic misfortunes. Vivid and painful memories of such shocks suffered by many countries in the 1930's were the prime mover in establishing an institution for "providing [members] with opportunity to correct maladjustments in their balance of payments without resorting to measures destructive of national or international prosperity", as Article I of the Fund Agreement puts it. Yet the disciplinary aspect was clearly recognized as well, as witness the intention of "making the Fund's resources temporarily available to [members] under adequate safeguards".

The Fund's resources are a revolving fund for mutual assistance on a continuing basis, not a source of grants or subsidies; drawings are intended to give a member time to devise and implement a constructive solution to the basic problem that underlies its balance-of-payments difficulties, whereupon they are to be repaid and thus made available to assist other members when needed. The inherent risks of misuse of the Fund's resources are obvious: not only the risk of inflation, which probably looked less serious when the opposite malady was so fresh in everyone's mind, but also the risk of depleting the Fund's resources and thereby threatening the world with a resumption of the beggar-my-neighbour policies of the 1930's. (How ironic that beggar-my-neighbour policies are again in fashion, this time because of the combination of inflation and unemployment instead of deflation and unemployment!)

Defence against misuse of the Fund's resources lies primarily with the Executive Directors, who must carefully review all requests for drawings in excess of a relatively modest portion of a member's quota.

Balancing the need to cushion economic adjustments within the economies of member nations against the risk of depleting the Fund's resources and contributing to world inflation is clearly a matter of judgment rather than precise calculation, and opinions about where the balance should be struck have clearly shifted over the years. And rightly so, as experience has accumulated. Standby arrangements were introduced in 1952, whereby a member may be assured of drawings in advance under agreed conditions and thereby enabled to plan ahead more effectively. In the same year the Fund modified its rules to assist in financing buffer stocks of primary commodities to stabilize their prices. Special facilities were introduced in 1963 for primary exporters faced with severe export shortfalls. In many other respects, too, procedures have been gradually liberalized over the years.

However, two important developments now in prospect merit careful scrutiny. First, it has been suggested that the size and distribution of current balance-of-payments deficits make it necessary to phase adjustments over a longer period of time. (At present a member is normally expected to repay the Fund within 3 to 5 years.) Second, it has been suggested that the Fund's lending limits (expressed as a percentage of each member's quota) should be expanded,* and that the Fund be permitted to borrow larger sums on world markets in order to increase its available resources. (It is already permitted to borrow from some member countries and from Switzerland.) But the size and the distribution of balance-of-payments deficits are themselves primarily reflections of the price and income distortions caused by inflation. Incautious moves in either of the directions suggested, let alone both at once, could seriously upset the present balance between the cushioning function of Fund lending and the inherent risks of destabilizing the world economy by encouraging further inflation.

Indeed, there are similar risks with the periodic review of Fund quotas in recognition of the expansion of world trade and world income. To the extent that this expansion is measured in monetary terms it is of course strongly influenced by the world-wide inflation that plagues us, and the increases in quotas are merely after-the-fact adjustments to rising prices. On the other hand there are important feedback effects: larger quotas

---

* This proposal has been turned down for the time being at least; in the negotiations for the increase in quotas that became effective in 1983 it was decided to **reduce** the percentages somewhat, because of the substantial increase in quotas.

cushion larger balance-of-payments deficits and thereby facilitate greater price increases than would otherwise occur. At present "reserve positions in the Fund" are a relatively small part of total international reserves (about 10 percent at the end of 1983), and their contribution to the increase over the past decade has been even smaller, so these feedback effects can not have been serious as yet.

Nevertheless there are ominous possibilities that some combination of larger quotas, larger drawings against quotas, and longer repayment periods may lead to the international equivalent of a national government stuffing its central bank with government debt and thereby generating major inflationary pressures. Note the following combination of circumstances: (1) Fund decisions are made either by its Executive Directors or by its Board of Governors; (2) each of these bodies is composed of representatives of member governments; and (3) under present circumstances most of these governments are actual or potential borrowers from the Fund, and therefore likely to be biased towards the cushioning aspects rather than the disciplinary aspects of their responsibilities. If the large and inflationary annual increments of international reserves now being generated by key-currency balance-of-payments deficits were to end, how would these debtor countries calculate their "need" for additional international reserves?

Chapter 14

WHAT *YOU* CAN DO

Is there anything the ordinary citizen can do to promote the search for a cure to inflation, or rather to The Fearsome Dilemma? Must he be content with weeping and wailing and gnashing his teeth, or is there anything positive he can do?

Yes, there are some positive things that can be done to help get politicians and economists (especially economists) off their chairs and actively searching for cures. They lie primarily in the field of mobilizing public opinion and making it known to the politicians and the economists, who must be directed to give first priority to this problem.

Your first step should be to make a summary in your own words of what you see to be the problem and how you think it should be attacked. This summary might be based entirely on what you have read in the preceding chapters of this book, though in all sincerity I would recommend that you do some additional reading as well—I am not so vain as to suppose that I can tell you all you need to know on the subject. Just what other articles and books you should read will depend on your familiarity with economics and what level of treatment you feel confident with. You may want to start with the article on inflation in any good encyclopaedia, though that will help you mostly with major inflations of the past and will not likely give you much help in understanding today's persistent world-wide inflation, and you must not expect to find anything there about The Fearsome Dilemma. In the References (beginning on page 185) you will find a few other readings that may be of help, though I hasten to add that I do not necessarily agree with every conclusion of every author nor with every policy they advocate.

You will find that making your summary will help to clarify things in your mind; it is a well-established principle that the best way to learn a subject is to teach it to someone else. When you have your summary complete, use it to get others interested. First, write letters to the editor of your local newspaper and to the editors of important regional and national newspapers. You may not want to use all the material in your summary for this, and may find it better to pick out what you think are the most persuasive points for your particular audience. Your letter will have to be long enough to make a reasonable case, but not so long that the editor will reject it for lack of space or (almost as bad) chop it down severely and lose the thread of your argument. Try to write in a way that will invite others to join in with letters of their own. If there are national magazines that invite letters to the editor, write them too.

Next, write to your political representatives—your member of parliament, your congressman and senator, or the equivalent in your country. Write also to other important political leaders, such as the Minister of Finance or the Secretary of the Treasury or other cabinet ministers, the chairman of the finance committee or board, the Prime Minister or the President, and the leaders of major political parties. Don't neglect the financial critics of opposition parties. The more letters you write the better. You will use your summary for these letters too, and you will be able to write at greater length and go into greater detail than in letters to the editor. A letter that shows evidence of serious thought and concern and clearly comes from an ordinary citizen will carry more weight than a glib letter from an expert.

Don't forget professional economists—they need prodding too. Write to the economics departments of universities and colleges, and to economic research institutions, describing your concerns and asking them to direct research to the problem. Write to as many of these institutions as you can—not all of them at once, for there are many of them, but a few at a time. That will help keep your own interest up, and if you are joined by others it will mean a continuing reminder to the academic community.

You may not get much immediate response from all these letters, though politicians will probably send you at least a polite acknowledgement. Don't despair. All these people are busy, and may not pay much attention to one individual, so encourage others to write as well. Talk it up among your friends. Try to form a discussion group that is willing to meet at stated intervals to support one another and to work out plans for influencing others. If you can't get a group of your friends together, or if your group wants to expand, take a bold step: put an advertisement in the "personals" column of the classified-advertisements section of your newspaper and of other newspapers and periodicals that offer this facility, and ask anyone else interested in understanding inflation and what we can do about it to get in touch with you.

Once you get a group going, or on your own if you feel brave enough, write to local service clubs and similar groups offering to provide a speaker at no cost (except repayment of any out-of-pocket expenses that may be involved) to talk about inflation and its cure. When you get a request to provide a speaker from among your group, have him stress what we (the general public) can **do** about inflation, rather than just talking about how bad it is—prodding political leaders to act, and prodding university economics faculties and economic research bodies to make the study of The Fearsome Dilemma a major priority.

Appendix

SELECTED ECONOMIC MODELS

1. The Uses and Abuses of Models

The economic forces at work in the real world and the agencies through which they operate are so numerous, and their interrelationships are so complex, that they must be reduced to a simplified schematic representation if they are to be even imperfectly comprehended by the human mind. These schematic representations are known as "models", and may be likened to the diagrams physical scientists use to explain the structure of a molecule or the workings of natural laws. Many similar but by-no-means-homogeneous entities must be lumped together and treated as one. To be blunt about it, even the best of these models are gross oversimplifications of reality. Nevertheless they can provide useful insights and useful policy guides when carefully used.

Any model must make some more-or-less-arbitrary assumptions about the working of the economy (or of that part of the economy it is primarily concerned with), in order to reduce the problem to manageable proportions. It must then identify those particular economic variables and forces that are deemed to be most significant for the purposes of the analysis, and will either ignore all other elements altogether or deem them to remain unchanged regardless of what happens within the confines of that particular model. Naturally, the assumptions and elements that are important for one purpose need not be significant for other purposes. It follows that two or more models may usefully supplement one another even though they do not make exactly the same assumptions, do not deal with exactly the same variables and forces, or do not define these elements in exactly the same way, as long as the assumptions and definitions are not actually contradictory, since each may illuminate a different facet of reality. Thus it is not necessarily valid to criticize a model for excluding certain factors that it does not explicitly address; it may well be that a supplementary model can show how consideration of the excluded elements modifies the conclusions of the original model.

More generally, the conclusions derived from **any** model are no better than the assumptions on which they are based—and some important assumptions may not be explicitly stated but merely implied. As with computer inputs and outputs, "Garbage in, garbage out!" All conclusions must therefore be carefully screened before being applied in the real world, and adjustments or qualifications made to allow for the effects of factors that have been ignored in the analysis. Perhaps the original model can be revised and expanded to take account of some of these factors, but perhaps the best that can be done is to make some sort of collective value judgment about how far the conclusions can be trusted. *Ceteris paribus* (other things remaining unchanged) assumptions are a valuable ally in economic analysis, for they permit the isolation of the effects of particular elements, but they are a treacherous foe in policy applications.

A major test of any model, of course, is how closely its explicit and implicit assumptions mirror the facts of life in the real world, for they uniquely determine the conclusions to be drawn from it. This raises the question of the proper trade-off between reality and tractability: the more realistic the model, the more complex and the less tractable it must be. Applying this test obviously involves value judgments about which opinions may validly differ by a wide margin. The most effective criticism of any model, therefore, is another model that is widely recognized as being more realistic yet that is not too complex for useful applications.

Most models of money-and-market economies are best understood in terms of a circular flow of money payments in one direction (the spending stream), which regulates a flow of goods and services in the opposite direction. As consumers spend their incomes for what they want, they in effect put command over productive resources in the hands of the sellers. These productive resources are classified into three major categories, known as factors of production: land (which stands for natural resources generally), labour, and capital goods (or just "capital" for short).* The payments received by the various agents of production (the providers of the services of these factors, i.e. individual labourers and individual parcels of land or of capital goods) or their owners constitute the income from which these same people as consumers purchase the goods and services they help to produce, thus completing the circular flow of money payments. Savings may be invested directly in new capital goods (as when a business firm reinvests a portion of its earnings), or may be made available through financial institutions and capital markets to others who wish to make larger investments than their own savings permit.

And now, before proceeding farther, a warning. Some writers wish to confine the term "model" to **econometric** models, i.e. those that are

---

* Sometimes a fourth category is identified, i.e. entrepreneurship—specialized skill in combining the other factors of production in efficient enterprises— but it is hard to specify where mere management ends and true entrepreneurship begins, so both are usually treated as special categories of labour. Also, though it may shock some purists, land may be treated as just a special category of capital goods, thus reducing the major factors of production to two.

formulated as a set of quantitative mathematical equations. This is not valid. Econometric models are not the only form, and do not necessarily give the best explanations of economic phenomena; they may yield quantitative answers to specific questions, but they risk becoming so rigid that any change in a major component (say, a change in official policy) requires a complete revision of the model. Literary models do not yield quantitative answers, but they may give a more-generally-useful account of economic relationships.

2. Pure Competition

Until 1933 the principal model available to economists and economic policymakers was the model of pure competition,[1] though separate models were also used to describe pure monopoly and certain other situations thought of as special cases. ("Pure" competition means no market participant has any semblance of monopolistic power, "pure" monopoly means the seller faces no competition in any form.) Every product is made in identical form by many competing producers and bought by many purchasers, no one of whom can influence the market price even if he withholds his entire supply or his entire demand. The factors of production share the total output in proportion to their respective marginal contributions (i.e. the additional output that can be attributed to the last unit of input of the factor that can be profitably employed, if all other inputs remain unchanged); and these shares are identical whether measured in physical units of output or in their money value, since the latter will be equal to the former multiplied by the market-fixed price.

Any producer can only increase his total revenue by selling more of his product at the market-fixed price; his cost of producing additional units will begin to rise sharply at some point, as his output approaches the maximum that can be squeezed out of his equipment; hence he will expand his output (and sales) until the point at which one more unit would cost more than it would sell for. Competition among producers will ensure that each operates with the most efficient size of plant, and that each plant is operated at its most efficient (lowest-cost) output. Competitive bidding for factors of production ensures that their returns are equalized in all employments, and that each is employed in its most fruitful applications (as measured by the demands registered by consumers in spending their incomes).

Each labourer balances the attractions of additional leisure against the goods and services he could obtain by working a little longer, to get equivalent satisfaction at the margin between work and leisure. The savings of savers and the physical investments of those who borrow for productive investments are kept in balance by the rate of interest: savers save more at higher interest rates, less at lower; the marginal product of capital goods, which determines what borrowers are willing to pay, declines as more is added; hence a rate of interest can be found that will just balance the marginal "cost" of saving (i.e. the satisfaction forgone by saving instead of consuming) with the marginal return to capital.

The full rigour of the model applies only in a long-run-equilibrium situation, which may be interpreted as arising at the end of an indefinitely-long period in which all existing disturbances or disequilibria can work themselves out and no new disturbances are allowed to occur. Shocks and disturbances of various kinds can indeed occur in the short run, but equilibrating forces will be set in motion automatically. Nevertheless certain short-run features of the model are essential to its operation, particularly the role of profits and the profit motive. "Profit" as used here does **not** mean or include normal returns to capital, which as we have just seen must equal the rate of interest in the long run, it means **pure** profit after the market rate of return has been paid to all factors of production. Typically, pure profit arises when an innovative entrepreneur pays the going rate of return to all factors of production but devises some new way of using them to create a new product or to produce an old product in a new and more-efficient way. It is strictly a short-run phenomenon, for imitators will surely adopt his methods; competition will then drive the price down until the pure profit disappears. This is the way the profit motive—the search for a pure profit—stimulates progress and spreads its benefits throughout the economy through new products and reduced prices.

The role of money in this model is relatively simple, adequately summarized by the so-called quantity theory of money (explained below). The relative prices of all goods and services are determined by the "real" forces operating in the economy, and the only thing money does is to settle the general price level. Of course sudden changes in the quantity of money do have disturbing temporary effects, but these work themselves out in the long run and "real" equilibrium is restored.

Two features of the model of pure competition merit special mention:

- The consumer is sovereign. His wishes and whims determine what will be produced and how the available resources will be used. There is no scope for advertizing or other selling expenses whereby the producer might influence the consumer, because all producers must sell common products at a market-fixed price price which can not exceed the factor costs of production by the most efficient known methods.
- Since all factors of production are used in the most efficient way for the satisfaction of human wants, the clear implication is that any interfer-

ence by the government or by any other body can only result in harm—with the exception, of course, of certain essential police, regulatory, and other functions.

One last point. We noted above that **pure** competition means that no monopolistic elements are present. However, other features of the real world may prevent the achievement of the optimum equilibrium position described in the model: frictions, lags, and similar impediments. A model that is free not only of monopolistic elements but also of these other impediments used to be known as exhibiting **perfect** competition—or sometimes "pure and perfect" competition, for those who wish to be meticulous. The two terms are often used interchangeably nowadays, and no great harm is done thereby, but the distinction seems still worth making.

3. General Equilibrium

The system depicted in the model of pure competition is a delicately-balanced complex of interacting forces, or what is technically known as a "general equilibrium" system. Simply stated, this means that "everything depends on everything else"—i.e. even a small change in any one element will affect all the other elements. For example, more of one product can only be produced by withdrawing resources from and therefore reducing the supply of some other product. Obviously such transfers of resources can not always be done quickly, but "in the long run" some old plants will not be replaced when they wear out and the resources that would have gone into replacing them will make capital available for other uses.

A general-equilibrium system may be likened to a set of simultaneous equations, in which the values of all unknowns are mutually determined. Some systems have indeed been set up in precisely this form, notably that of Léon Walras, a 19th-century mathematical economist. However, there are difficulties at both the theoretical level and the practical level in trying to deal with everything at once. Given the complexities of market interrelationships and the unavoidable lags before developments in one market can influence transactions in other markets, how can things ever sort themselves out and reach their long-run-equilibrium positions? Walras solved the problem at the theoretical level by an ingenious device: he had an auctioneer call out prices in each market, whereupon sellers indicated how much they would offer at that price and buyers how much they would take; if a market did not clear (supply and demand were unequal) at that price, a new price was called out; no sales were actually made until all markets were cleared in this way, whereupon all transactions were finalized simultaneously. It is obvious that this device has no relationship to how markets operate in the real world, and was never intended to do so; it is merely a way of telescoping the process of adjustment towards the equilibrium position.

The practical difficulties of dealing with all the variables at once have led to an alternative procedure, **particular** equilibrium analysis, which deals with equilibrium in a single market independently.* A curve or schedule or function is used to represent the amount that sellers would offer at various prices in a given situation, and another curve or schedule or function to represent the amount buyers would take. This is the commonly-used supply-and-demand analysis; the price that equates the two is the equilibrium price. If it is taken to represent a long-run situation, then it is only valid for very small departures of demand, supply, or price from the equilibrium position, so that any effect on the output and price of any other product is less than the acceptable margin of error in the analysis; long-run equilibrium in every particular market means long-run general equilibrium, and *vice versa*. If the particular-equilibrium model is used to represent a short-run situation—say, a period in which it is not feasible either to expand the existing physical plant or to convert it to other uses—then these limitations are somewhat reduced; however, if the short-run equilibrium position differs materially from the long-run position that would be appropriate to the existing conditions, then resources must sooner or later be diverted from this particular market to other markets, or the other way around. Hence, in principle at least, particular-equilibrium analysis is perfectly compatible with general-equilibrium analysis; they are linked by the dynamic process by which disturbances or disequilibria are deemed to work themselves out.

4. The Quantity Theory of Money and the Equation of Exchange

What is commonly known as the quantity theory of money is not a theory of money at all, but a quantity-of-money theory of prices. Rather than buck established usage, however, we may call it "the quantity theory of money and prices" or simply "the quantity theory". It is incorporated in the model of pure competition, but it also constitutes an important submodel in its own right.

---

* Particular-equilibrium analysis is an example of partial-equilibrium analysis, in which a given subset of variables is deemed to come into equilibrium subject to the constraint that the excluded variables are deemed to be held constant. Partial and general equilibrium may be compared to partial and total differentiation in differential calculus.

Following the version popularized by Irving Fisher early in the 20th-century [2] (there are several other versions as well, but they amount to the same thing), the theory begins with the assertion that the general price level varies directly as the quantity of money in circulation, directly as the velocity with which it turns over (i.e. the number of times each unit is spent on the average in a given period), and inversely as the volume of transactions effected. However, this is merely an introductory framework which has no theoretical content as such: it is simply an expression in plain language of a relationship that is said to exist among four variables, which is known as **the equation of exchange** and is usually expressed algebraically. Whether it is true or not depends on how the variables are defined, and can be empirically tested. The substance of **the theory** is that (subject to the qualifications noted below) the price level is passive and is determined by independent changes in the other variables.

Using P, M, V, and T for the four variables, as Fisher does, we can easily derive his algebraic version of the equation of exchange (there are others too, related to alternative versions of the quantity theory). His plain-language statement may be written $P \propto MV/T$, or $P = kMV/T$ where k is an arbitrary constant whose value depends on the units used. It is customary to use units which make $k = 1$, so the equation reduces to $P = MV/T$ or $MV = PT$. The four variables are sometimes defined in a way that makes the equation an identity ($MV \equiv PT$), but alternatively they may be defined in a way that makes it an equilibrating condition. For example, V may be identified with debits to chequeing accounts and T with some measure of the volume of transactions effected; or PT may be identified with the value of those transactions. Of course the definitions of M, V, P, and T must be consistent: V must refer to transactions effected with M, and any transactions excluded from T must also be excluded when computing V.*

To repeat, the essence of the quantity theory is that prices are the passive or dependent variable. It is fully applicable only in a long-run-equilibrium situation; in the short run there may be some feedback effects from prices on the other variables. The final-equilibrium value of T is identified with what we would now call the full-employment level of economic activity, since in the model of pure competition unemployment is a temporary short-run phenomenon. Similarly, V approaches a fixed

---

* This formulation of the equation of exchange is usually identified with the transactions version, in which T means all transactions effected by the transfer of money, including the purchase and sale of all intermediate goods as well as final products. However, it can be modified to apply to real income or output, or consumption goods, or other more limited interpretations.

or constant equilibrium value that is determined by payment practices and other institutional features of the economy. These equilibrium values may of course change gradually over time, due mainly to economic growth in the first case and changing habits and institutions in the second. Nevertheless, if you could stop all new initiatives in the model at any given point in time and let the equilibrating forces work themselves out, both would approach determinate fixed values (i.e. would become constants); prices would vary directly with the quantity of money.

Few if any economists now think this relatively-simple version of the quantity theory is very useful for explaining current economic events, though it has not entirely outlived its usefulness; for example, it is useful in explaining the effects of a sharp increase in the money supply, as when Europe experienced a great inflow of gold and silver after the discovery of the New World.

The equation of exchange, on the other hand, continues to be a useful shorthand device for describing the interactions of money and prices, without necessarily implying that the latter always responds passively to changes in the former. There are numerous versions, some of which come in several variations. One version introduces the so-called income-velocity of money, V_y, the rate at which money spent out of income returns again on the average as income. It is often written $MV_y = Y$, where Y means income and may be identified with gross national product or net national income or the like. In some variants income velocity is **defined** as the ratio of income to the money supply, so the equation becomes an indentity, $MV_y \equiv Y$; this is just a transposition of the definition, however, and offers no help in explaining how income or prices or other macroeconomic variables are determined, since a definition can not explain anything except the object defined. However, other variants identify income velocity independently, in which case the equation remains a useful equilibrating condition; see for example the monetarist formulation described in section 7. In all these variants it should be noted that prices either do not appear at all or else appear only as a component of some other variable.

5. Imperfect (or Monopolistic) Competition

As already noted, the model of pure competition recognizes that various frictions, lags, and other features of the real world may interfere with the attainment of the final equilibrium position; however, these features do not alter the optimum position to which the model tends, so they do not in any sense discredit it. Two books published independently in 1933 introduced an entirely new model in which the ultimate equilibrium position is very different: Edward Chamberlin's *The Theory of Monopolistic Competition*, and Joan Robinson's *The Economics of Imperfect Competition*. The two books take quite different approaches, but between them they delineate a schematic representation in which all other models from pure competition to pure monopoly can be included.

The operation of the economy is still best understood in terms of the circular flow of money payments in one direction and products in the opposite direction, but the operative forces are very different. Product differentiation (branded goods identified as the product of a particular seller, regardless of whether they differ materially from the branded goods of competing sellers) and other sales techniques permit sellers to create consumer loyalty and thus make their products wholly or partly immune to price competition; the consumer is not sovereign, but is badgered, confused, mesmerized, and misled by powerful and insidious advertizing campaigns and other devices. The resources at the disposal of a given seller do not reflect an objective valuation of their wants by the consumers themselves, but the skill of the seller in cajoling buyers or playing on their fears and vanities, or in gaining and exploiting some tactical advantage over his competitors. Factor returns are not proportionate to their marginal contribution to physical output, and are not necessarily equalized in all employments, but may vary from firm to firm and from industry to industry according to the bargaining strengths of each pair of buyers and sellers.

Most producers will find that progressively larger sales in a given situation will require progressively lower selling prices; each additional unit sold will add less than its selling price to total revenue, because it will require a slightly lower markup on all sales (marginal revenue is less than average revenue per unit sold). Instead of expanding sales until the cost of the last unit sold (marginal cost) just equals the market-fixed selling price, as in the model of pure competition, producers will try to limit their sales to the somewhat lower level at which marginal revenue just covers marginal cost.

The policy implications of this model are quite different from those of the model of pure competition. There is no assurance that the community's resources are being employed in the most efficient way for the satisfaction of human wants: on the contrary, there is every reason to believe that resources will be wasted in unnecessary duplication of plants that will not be used to their full capacity. There is no basis for supposing that the benefits of innovations and cost reductions will be passed on to the general public in the form of price reductions; instead, they are likely to go to those factors of production that have the greatest bargaining strength and are most willing to exploit it. There is no clear presumption against government interference in economic affairs; on the contrary, it appears that certain kinds of intervention would shift output and prices towards the levels that would obtain under pure competition and thereby spread the benefits of progress more evenly among the members of the general public.

6. Keynesian Economics

Another new economic model began to evolve with the publication of J.M. Keynes's *The General Theory of Employment, Interest, and Money* in 1936. The term "Keynesian" is used in many different senses, ranging from what Keynes himself said between the covers of that one book through what various individual disciples have thought he meant (or thought he should have said) to something generally known by professional economists as "post-Keynesianism", i.e. a general body of principles that has gradually evolved over the ensuing years and incorporates many elaborations and modifications by other economists. But "post-Keynesianism" is unsatisfactory for general usage, because there are continuing disagreements (which may never be fully resolved to everyone's satisfaction) over certain details that seem very important to the protagonists; indeed, some schools of thought wish to restrict the term to their own particular version of the doctrine. It therefore seems best to use "Keynesian" as a generic term, and to interpret it as including post-Keynesianism, neo-Keynesianism, and other varieties however defined.

The Keynesian economic model differs from both the model of pure competition and the model of imperfect (or monopolistic) competition in two important respects. First, it is addressed to broad economic categories like the total output of the economy (which is equal to total income, and may be measured in either current monetary terms or in physical terms valued at the prices of some base period), total employment, total savings, total investment in new capital installations, and the like, rather than to individual products, firms, and industries. In technical terms it is a macroeconomic model, whereas the models of pure competition and imperfect (or monopolistic) competition are microeconomic. Second, it is addressed to relatively short-run conditions—the sort of timeframe in which current economic policies must be formulated and implemented. In its simplest form it focuses on just four variables: total output or total income (Y), consumption (C), savings (S), and investment or new capital formation (I) in a given period of time. Income is generated by total spending on consumption and investment, and is disposed of by either being spent on consumption or being saved, all of which may be expressed algebraically as $C + I = Y = C + S$.

Obviously, new investment must be financed out of savings ($I = S$); but the rate of interest does not suffice to bring this about, as it does in the model of pure competition (and presumably in the model of imperfect or monopolistic competition as well), because there is no presumption that the amount of saving is materially influenced by the rate of interest and because the rate of interest is neither the only nor even the most important factor influencing investment decisions. Instead, the operation of the system is governed by three psychological factors: the propensity to consume (and its complement, the propensity to save), savers' desires for liquidity as well as earnings (liquidity preference), and investors' expectations of net earnings on new capital goods. All three are potentially volatile in the face of purely psychological influences, but especially the last two; the propensity to consume (or to save) is thought to be relatively stable at any given level of income, but proportionately more is saved as income rises.* Interest is seen as the price that must be paid to induce savers to acquire less-liquid assets such as bonds instead of holding cash. New investment depends on an expectation that the rate of return will exceed the interest costs that must be incurred or the interest earnings that must be forgone in order to make the investment (there must be a positive "inducement to invest"). Wages and prices are resistant (sticky) in the face of downward pressures, though free to rise if the opportunity offers, hence a reduction in the money supply will not be very effective in reducing prices or wages, and a surplus of supply in any market will not automatically clear itself.

Chronic unemployment is impossible in the model of pure competition. If new investment declines for any reason, saving will also decline by the same amount and the spending stream will be sustained by increased consumption. If some temporary unemployment does appear, wages will fall in both real and money terms until the labour supply is again fully employed. (Strictly speaking, of course, these adjustments only occur in the long run; however, we may infer that an older generation of economists thought the equilibrating forces acted pretty quickly, for they freely prescribed purely-competitive remedies for all current problems.) Pretty much the same applies to the model of imper-

---

* Consumption is related to income by the consumption function. Consumption is usually represented as greater than income at low levels of income, but less than income at high levels of income. In general, any increment of income is represented as giving rise to a somewhat-smaller increment of consumption and a considerably-smaller increment of savings.

fect or monopolistic competition; the labour freed by below-capacity operations is not unemployed, it merely shifts to otherwise-marginal productive activities.

In contrast, chronic unemployment is quite possible in the Keynesian model—its very origin was to explain that phenomenon, which was all too obvious in the real world but could not be explained by existing economic models. If investment falls below the level of savings being generated at the current level of income, then output, employment, and income will fall until the (smaller) savings generated at the now-reduced level of income are fully absorbed to finance new investment—and of course the amount of investment that investors are now prepared to make will be even smaller than before, because the lower level of economic activity will reduce the need for additional capital. Wages (and prices) will not fall appreciably, so labour (and other) markets will not clear automatically: labour and other resources will be unemployed or underemployed.

Changes in real and money income, not changes in interest rates and prices, become the equilibrating element. A reduction in interest rates, fostered by monetary expansion, **may** encourage some new investment by reducing its cost, but it is more likely that the inducement to invest will be negative for most businessmen due to the decline in sales volume. If the economy is left to "natural" forces, therefore, recovery will not occur until a good deal of existing capital equipment is worn out and needs replacing. But new government spending may substitute for private investment and thus qualify as "honourary investment", either for the purchase of goods and services (say, public works) or for the support of the incomes of the unemployed and underemployed; or the government may cut taxes and thereby stimulate increased private consumption. An essential part of the process, of course, is an equivalent increase in the government's deficit, so that its borrowing will absorb the savings that would otherwise be lost along with the income lost through unemployment. (It is **not** necessary that the deficit be financed by monetary expansion; market issues will do just as well. Since a relatively easy monetary policy is a logical complement to an expansionary fiscal policy in many circumstances, however, the banking system may well absorb a good deal of the new issues.)

Parenthetically, we may note that the Keynesian model is quite compatible with either the model of pure competition or the model of imperfect (monopolistic) competition, subject to rather moderate changes in the older models, for it is a relatively-short-run model whereas they are primarily long-run models. Keynes viewed himself as an amender, not a rejector, of classical purely-competitive theory, and made no reference to the then-very-recent works of Chamberlin and Robinson; subsequent contributors have pretty much followed his lead, though at the very least the newer versions of competition would help to explain the stickiness of prices and wages that Keynes emphasized. There is nothing in the Keynesian model to deny the existence of an equilibrating mechanism **tending** toward a full-employment equilibrium in the long run; all that is necessary is the postulate that such a result is not reached quickly and automatically. It may well be, for example, that the real-world equivalent of "exogenous shocks" (disturbances from outside the system) are of such magnitude and occur with such frequency that a relatively-slowly-operating adjustment mechanism is continually being thwarted. Keynes's oft-quoted quip that "in the long run we are all dead" does not deny the possibility of a long-run equilibrium, it merely implies that any such possibility is irrelevant for current policy decision-making: we **can't** wait that long, because the "cure" won't help the dead, and we **needn't** wait, because there are things we can do that should bring quick relief.

The demand-management techniques that gained favour after World War II are based on more sophisticated versions of the Keynesian model than the simple one outlined above,* but the same principles apply. If aggregate spending is too low and unemployment threatens, monetary policy may be used to reduce interest rates or to keep them low, in an effort to encourage more capital formation. In addition, government spending may be increased or taxes reduced, and the deficit covered by borrowing, thus maintaining the spending stream and supporting incomes and employment. If on the other hand aggregate spending gets too vigourous and inflationary pressures appear, government spending may be cut back and taxes raised; if necessary, monetary policy can be tightened and interest rates raised until the rate of new capital formation is reduced to the level that can be financed out of the current level of savings. To some extent these results will be brought about automatically by built-in stabilizers: unemployment-insurance claims and other social expenditures will rise or fall as unemployment rises or falls, and tax revenues will fall or rise as the general level of economic activity falls

---

* For example, the spending categories that generate income may be enlarged to include government spending on goods and services and exports purchased by foreign customers as well as domestic spending on consumer goods and investment goods. (Government support for personal incomes, as from unemployment-insurance funds, is included in consumer spending.) Similarly, the ways in which income can be disposed of may be enlarged to include the payment of taxes to the government and the purchase of imports as well as saving and spending on domestically-produced consumer goods and services.

or rises. Unfortunately, however, a serious weakness in this prescription has emerged in recent years, as noted in the second section of Chapter 7: it can not deal effectively with either unemployment or inflation when they arise simultaneously.

7. Monetarism

Monetarism, like the quantity theory of money from which it is directly descended, is not a theory of money but a theory about money. Its principal advocate is Milton Friedman, and its starting-point is a reassertion of the importance of money in economic affairs. Keynes had argued that, in a deep depression, a point might be reached at which further expansion of the money supply would bring no further reduction in interest rates because people would merely add it to their money balances instead of using it to acquire more earning assets (the so-called "liquidity trap"), and in the 1950's some of his disciples seemed to have reduced the role of money to the vanishing point. In 1956 Friedman published a restatement of the quantity theory,[3] which insisted on the importance of money but nevertheless ascribed strictly limited powers to monetary policy. He enlarged on these views in subsequent writings, and in 1969 Karl Brunner christened the revised theory "monetarism".

According to Friedman, monetarism is in the first instance a theory of the demand for money, not a theory of output or money income or prices. Money is an asset, i.e. an alternative way of holding wealth, and yields productive services. The demand for it depends primarily on total wealth ("the budget constraint"), on the returns from or the services rendered by money itself, on the returns yielded by alternative assets, and on the tastes and preferences of wealth-holders. From this he derives a schematic representation in which the demand for money is determined by the interest rate, the rate of return on equities, wealth, income, and other factors. The mathematical equation used to express these relationships can be rewritten in a form that is equivalent to the income version of the equation of exchange, $MV_y = Y$, in which V_y becomes a function of the rate of interest, the rate of return on equities, prices, wealth, and a number of other variables.

Friedman believes that most economists could accept the general lines of this approach readily enough, though there would be fundamental differences of opinion about its importance for understanding general economic activity. He defines a quantity theorist (i.e. a monetarist) in terms of three beliefs: (1) He accepts the empirical hypothesis that the demand for money is stable—more stable than the consumption function, for example. (2) He rejects the thesis that a change in the demand for money may call forth a corresponding change in the supply. (3) He denies that a liquidity-trap situation may arise, and that the role of money is merely to determine the rate of interest. These beliefs directly contradict views widely held by professing Keynesians.

Even though these propositions about money are the source of monetarism's name, however, they are not the main distinguishing feature of its analytical structure. Friedman is surely right that most economists could accept his framework as a basis for analysis. Furthermore, Keynesians and others could probably learn to live with themselves if empirical studies showed convincingly that all three of Friedman's definitional beliefs were valid—contrary views are conspicuous in much Keynesian writing, but they are not essential to an underemployment equilibrium nor to Keynesian policy prescriptions. What really separates monetarist from nonmonetarist thought, as Friedman himself points out, is a very different set of basic assumptions about how the economy operates. Monetarists retain a firm belief in a market system that closely resembles the model of perfect competition, except for replacing the old version of the quantity theory with the monetarist version: wages and prices are flexible; markets clear, apparently rather quickly; unemployment is largely voluntary, i.e. workers prefer more leisure rather than more work at the going wage rates.

One of the most obvious and important aspects of the philosophical orientation of monetarism is its insistence that economic decisions are taken primarily in terms of "real" economic considerations, not nominal or merely-monetary considerations. Thus in 1967 Friedman argued that the monetary authorities can control the exchange rate, the price level, the nominal level of income, the quantity of money however one chooses to define it, and other **nominal** quantities.[4] They can thereby prevent money itself from being a source of disturbance (e.g., by bringing on an unnecessary deflation), and can provide a stable economic environment; perhaps they can also help correct **major** disturbances, though it is doubtful that this can be kept within proper bounds. However, the authorities can not control **real** quantities—unemployment, real interest rates, real income, or the like. Monetary policy may indeed effect temporary changes in them, but natural equilibrating forces will then assert themselves. Thus there is a "natural" level of interest rates (an idea that goes back into the 19th century): attempting to keep market rates below the natural rate means expanding the money supply, which sets in motion forces that increase the spending stream, loan demand, money income, and perhaps prices, and will ultimately raise interest rates back up to their natural level. Similarly, Friedman postulates a "natural" level of unemployment; any departure from it will set forces in motion that will restore it.

Friedman argues that any changes in real quantities after a change in the money supply are attributable to imperfect information and are therefore temporary. Actual unemployment can not permanently differ from the natural rate without a continuous acceleration or deceleration of the growth of the money supply. Suppose the economy is initially in equilibrium, but the government erroneously believes there is involuntary unemployment and increases the money supply to increase output. Demand for real output will indeed increase, and will cause inflation to accelerate. Money wages will rise more slowly than prices, as wage-earners do not at once see what is happening. Employers will realize that real wages have fallen, however, and will wish to hire more people. Some of the **voluntarily**-unemployed will offer their services, because they have been fooled into believing that real wages have risen, so output will rise; but they will soon see their error and withdraw their services. Real wages, output, and employment will return to their old levels, but the inflation rate will now be higher.

Just as "Keynesianism" may be interpreted as including a variety of versions that differ in their details in ways that are of more interest to the specialist than to the general reader, so with "monetarism". One important variant is sometimes called "the new classical economics".[5] To the standard monetarist postulates (1) that economic decisions are made in real not nominal terms and (2) that economic agents are continuously in equilibrium within their given level of information, this version adds (3) that economic agents make no systematic errors and rationally project the future on the basis of all the available facts, including changes in official policies (the "rational expectations" assumption). This third postulate implies that economic expectations are appropriate to the structure of the economic model, and that no-one can obtain an advantage from a correct forecast unless it is based on information not available to others. The net result is that in this version there can not be even temporary departures from equilibrium. "Full information" becomes the means of achieving an economic optimum.

References

REFERENCES

Chapter 1: THE ATTRIBUTES OF INFLATION

Chapter 2: LESSONS FROM THE PAST
[1] F.D. Graham, *Exchange, Prices, and Production in Hyper-Inflation,* p. 67.
[2] R.G. Hawtrey, *Currency and Credit,* p. 428.
[3] G. Haberler, *Inflation,* p. 57.

* * *

Alden, John R. *The American Revolution 1775-1783.* London; H. Hamilton, 1954.
Angell, Norman. *The Story of Money.* London; Cassell, 1930.
Dewey, Davis R. *Financial History of the U.S.* New York; Longmans Green, 1903.
Galbraith, John K. *Money.* New York; Bantam, 1976.
Graham, Frank D. *Exchange, Prices, and Production in Hyper-Inflation: Germany, 1920-23.* Princeton, N.J.; Princeton University Press, 1930.
Haberler, Gottfried. *Inflation: Its Causes and Cures.* Washington; American Enterprise Institute for Public Policy Research, 1966.
Hawtrey, Ralph G. *Currency and Credit.* London and New York; Longmans Green, 1930.
Laursen, Karsten, and Pedersen, Jörgen. *The German Inflation 1918-23.* Amsterdam; North-Holland, 1964.
Morison, Samuel E., and Carnnoger, Henry S. *The Growth of the American Republic.* New York; Oxford University Press, 5th ed., 1962.
Viner, Jacob. *Studies in the Theory of International Trade.* New York and London; Harper, 1937. [Technical.]
Wood, Elmer. *English Theories of Central Banking 1819-1858.* Cambridge, Mass.; Harvard University Press,1939. [Technical.]

Chapter 3: THE ROLE OF MONEY IN INFLATION
[1] A good place to start would be with Friedman's Wincott Memorial Lecture, *The Counter-Revolution in Monetary Theory.* Many of his other works are addressed to the specialist, but his presidential address to the American Economic Association in December 1967, entitled "The Role of Monetary Policy", is fairly straightforward. Other monetarist writers include Karl Brunner, Phillip Cagan, Harry Johnson, David Laidler, David Meiselman, Allan H. Meltzer, and Anna Schwartz. [Most of these writings are technical.]
[2] I. Fisher, *The Purchasing Power of Money,* p.71. Transition periods are discussed in Chapter IV, pp. 55-73.
[3] J.M. Keynes, *The Economic Consequences of the Peace.*

* * *

Fisher, Irving. *The Purchasing Power of Money.* New York; 2nd rev. ed.,1922, reprinted by Augustus M. Kelley, 1963. [Technical.]
Friedman, Milton. *The Counter-Revolution in Monetary Theory.* London; Institute of Economic Affairs, Occasional Paper 33, 1970.
_____. "The Role of Monetary Policy", *The American Economic Review,* Vol. 58, no. 1, March 1978, pp. 1-17.
Graham, Frank D. As listed for Chapter 2.
Hawtrey, Ralph G. As listed for Chapter 2.
Keynes, J. Maynard. *The Economic Consequences of the Peace.* New York; Harcourt Brace,1920.

Chapter 4: **EXTERNAL ASPECTS**
Friedman, Milton. "The Euro-Dollar Market: Some First Principles", *The Morgan Guaranty Survey*, October 1969.
Triffin, Robert. *Europe and the Money Muddle: From Bilateralism to Near-Convertibility, 1947-1956.* New Haven, Conn.; Yale University Press,1957.
_____. *Gold and the Dollar Crisis: The Future of Convertibility.* New Haven, Conn.; Yale University Press, rev. ed.,1961.
_____. *The World Money Maze: National Currencies in International Payments.* New Haven, Conn.; Yale University Press,1966.
_____. "'Europe and the Money Muddle' Revisited", *Banca Nazionale del Lavoro Quarterly Review*, No. 124, March 1978.

Chapter 5: **THE MICROECONOMICS OF INFLATION**
Slawson, W. David. *The New Inflation: The Collapse of Free Markets.* Princeton, N.J.; Princeton University Press, 1981.

Chapter 6: **REAL-WORLD PRICING**
[1] W.J. Stanton, *Fundamentals of Marketing,* p.5.
[2] The same work, pp. 545-551.

* * *

Stanton, William J. *The Fundamentals of Marketing.* New York; McGraw-Hill, 1964.

Chapter 7: **THE MACROECONOMICS OF INFLATION**
[1] J. Tinbergen, *On the Theory of Economic Policy; Centralization and Decentralization in Economic Policy;* and *Economic Policy: Principles and Dangers.*
[2] J. Cornwall and W. Maclean, *Economic Recovery for Canada*, p. 18.
[3] M. Lamontagne, *Business Cycles in Canada.*

* * *

Cornwall, John, and Maclean, Wendie. *Economic Recovery for Canada: A Policy Framework.* Ottawa; Canadian Institute for Economic Policy, 1984.
Friedman, Milton. As listed for Chapter 3.
Lamontagne, Maurice. *Business Cycles in Canada.* Ottawa; Canadian Institute for Economic Policy, 1984.
Tinbergen, Jan. *On the Theory of Economic Policy.* North-Holland, 1952. [Technical.]
_____. *Centralization and Decentralization in Economic Policy.* Amsterdam, North-Holland, 1954. [Technical.]
_____. *Economic Policy: Principles and Dangers.* Amsterdam, North-Holland, 1956. [Technical.]

Chapter 8: **THE REDISTRIBUTION OF INCOME**
Maddison, Angus. "Origins and Impact of the Welfare State, 1883-1983", *Banca Nazionale del Lavoro Quarterly Review*, No. 148, March 1984, pp. 55-87.
Peterson, Wallace C. *Our Overloaded Economy.* Armonk, N.Y.; M.E. Sharpe, 1982.
Rotstein, Abraham. *Rebuilding from Within: Remedies for Canada's Ailing Economy.* Ottawa; Canadian Institute for Economic Policy, 1984.

Chapter 9: **A LOSING STRATEGY**

[1] In his address to the annual meeting of the of the Fund in 1982, and in subsequent statements.

[2] For a different viewpoint on these problems see "The Growth of Public Debt" by Mr. de Larosière.

* * *

de Larosière, J. "The Growth of Public Debt and the Need for Fiscal Discipline" (an address to the Fortieth Congress of the International Institute for Public Finance in Innsbruck, Austria, on 27th August 1984), *IMF Survey*, 3rd September 1984, pp. 261-268.

Chapter 10: **OTHER INEFFECTIVE REMEDIES**

[1] S. Weintraub and H.C. Wallich, "A Tax-Based Incomes Policy", and S. Weintraub, "Proposals for an Anti-Inflation Policy". Others have offered variants, or have made similar proposals.

[2] A.P. Lerner, "The Market Antiinflation Plan".

* * *

Friedman, Milton. As listed for Chapter 3.

Gapinski, James H., and Rockwood, Charles E., eds. *Essays in Post-Keynesian Inflation*. Cambridge, Mass.; Ballinger, 1979.

Lerner, Abba P. "The Market Antiinflation Plan: A Cure for Stagflation", in J.H. Gapinski and C.E. Rockwood (eds.), *Essays in Post-Keynesian Inflation,* pp. 217-229.

Weintraub, Sidney, and Wallich, Henry C. "A Tax-Based Incomes Policy", *Journal of Economic Issues*, Vol. V, no. 2, June 1971, pp. 1-19.

Weintraub, Sidney. "Proposals for an Anti-Inflation Policy", *Challenge*, Vol. 21, no. 4, September/October 1978, pp. 53- 54.

Chapter 11: **A WINNING STRATEGY**

[1] J.M. Keynes, *The Economic Consequences of Mr. Churchill*, originally published by Hogarth Press in London in 1925; reprinted in *Essays in Persuasion*, pp. 244-287.

* * *

Keynes, J. Maynard. *Essays in Persuasion*. London; Macmillan, 1931.

Chapter 12: **OTHER GOVERNMENT INTERVENTIONS**

[1] "[L]e travail ne peut être une loi sans être un droit"; *Les Misérables*, Vol. III, p. 27 [Fourth Part, Seventh Book, IV].

* * *

Hugo, Victor M. *Les Misérables*. Paris; Le Livre de Poche, 1972.

Petersen, Wallace C. As listed for Chapter 8.

Chapter 13: **THE INTERNATIONAL FIELD**

[1] R. Triffin, *Europe and the Money Muddle, Gold and the Dollar Crisis, The World Money Maze*, and other writings.

[2] *Business Week*, 30th June 1980, pp. 55-142.

* * *

International Monetary Fund, Washington, D.C., Pamphlet Series: No. 1 (*Introduction to the Fund*, by J. Keith Horsefield, 2nd. ed., 1965), No. 17 (*The Reform of the Fund*, by Joseph Gold, 1969), No. 25 (*The Second Amendment to the Articles of Agreement*, by Joseph Gold, 1978), and No. 37 (*The International Monetary Fund: Its Evolution, Organization, and Activities*, by Augustus W. Hooke, 1981).

Triffin, Robert. As listed for Chapter 4.

Chapter 14: **WHAT *YOU* CAN DO**

Appendix: **SELECTED ECONOMIC MODELS**

[1] See any good introductory textbook in economics, such as the most recent available edition of P.A. Samuelson's *Economics* or R.G. Lipsey and P.O. Steiner's *Economics*.

[2] *The Purchasing Power of Money*. Most introductory economics textbooks summarize the theory, though not always adequately.

[3] "The Quantity Theory of Money: A Restatement".

[4] Presidential address to the American Economic Association, "The Role of Monetary Policy".

[5] See, for example, K.D. Hoover, "Two Types of Monetarism".

* * *

Chamberlin, Edward H. *The Theory of Monopolistic Competition*. Cambridge, Mass.; Harvard University Press, 6th ed., 1950 [1st ed. 1933]. [Technical.]

Fisher, Irving. As listed for Chapter 3.

Friedman, Milton. As listed for Chapter 3.

_____. "The Quantity Theory of Money: A Restatement", in *Studies in the Quantity Theory of Money*, M. Friedman (ed.), Chicago, University of Chicago Press, 1956. [Technical.]

Hoover, Kevin D. "Two Types of Monetarism", *Journal of Economic Literature*, Vol. XXII, no. 1, March 1984, pp. 58-76.

Keynes, J. Maynard. *The General Theory of Employment, Interest, and Money*. London; Macmillan, 1936. [Technical. Most introductory economics textbooks provide an adequate summary of his model.]

Lipsey, Richard G., and Steiner, Peter O. *Economics*. New York; Harper & Row, 6th ed., 1981.

Robertson, Dennis H. *Money*. London; Nisbit, 4th ed., 1948.

Robinson, Joan. *The Economics of Imperfect Competition*. London; Macmillan, 1933. [Technical.]

Samuelson, Paul A. *Economics*. New York; McGraw-Hill, 11th ed., 1980.

ABOUT THE AUTHOR

ALEXANDER NORMAN McLEOD, B.A., M.P.A., Ph.D., is a monetary economist who is experienced in practical applications as well as in theoretical developments. He had a distinguished academic career, being medalist at Queen's University, Littauer Fellow at Harvard, and later a professor at Atkinson College of York University in Toronto, from which he retired in 1977 as Professor Emeritus.

Between these academic periods A.N.M. pursued the practical application of theory. He was an early staff member of the International Monetary Fund, which sent him to several Central American countries on financial missions and in 1950-51 seconded him as a monetary adviser to the United Nations Commissioner in Libya in preparation for independence. On leave from the Fund, he was Director of Research for the Saudi Arabian Monetary Agency for two years. Later (1966-69) the Fund's Central Banking Service provided him to Trinidad and Tobago as Governor of that country's central bank. In the meantime he was Chief Economist of The Toronto-Dominion Bank for ten years, and established its Research Department. During that period he was chairman of the Economists' Committee of the Canadian Bankers' Association, which drafted the Association's influential presentation to the Royal Commission on Banking and Finance (the Porter Commission). York University gave him a leave of absence in 1973 to advise the Government of Botswana on monetary matters, which led to the establishment of their central bank.

Married, with four sons and a growing assortment of grandchildren, Professor McLeod now writes and works in support of national and international policies that are both socially responsible and economically sound.

189

Index

Index